powerful
thinking

JOYCE MEYER

New York • Nashville

FaithWords
Hachette Book Group
1290 Avenue of the Americas, New York, NY 10104
faithwords.com
twitter.com/faithwords

First Edition: June 2021

FaithWords is a division of Hachette Book Group, Inc. The FaithWords name and logo are trademarks of Hachette Book Group, Inc.

The publisher is not responsible for websites (or their content) that are not owned by the publisher.

The Hachette Speakers Bureau provides a wide range of authors for speaking events. To find out more, go to www.hachettespeakersbureau.com or call (866) 376-6591.

Unless otherwise noted, Scripture quotations are taken from the Holy Bible, New International Version®, NIV®. Copyright ©1973, 1978, 1984, 2011 by Biblica, Inc.™ Used by permission of Zondervan. All rights reserved worldwide. www.zondervan.com The "NIV" and "New International Version" are trademarks registered in the United States Patent and Trademark Office by Biblica, Inc.™ | Scripture quotations marked AMPC are taken from the Amplified® Bible, Copyright © 1954, 1958, 1962, 1964, 1965, 1987 by The Lockman Foundation Used by permission. www.Lockman.org. | Scripture quotations marked NKJV are taken from the New King James Version®. Copyright © 1982 by Thomas Nelson. Used by permission. All rights reserved. | Scripture quotations marked MSG are taken from THE MESSAGE, copyright © 1993, 2002, 2018 by Eugene H. Peterson. Used by permission of NavPress. All rights reserved. Represented by Tyndale House Publishers, a Division of Tyndale House Ministries. | Scripture quotations marked ESV are from the ESV® Bible (The Holy Bible, English Standard Version®), copyright © 2001 by Crossway, a publishing ministry of Good News Publishers. Used by permission. All rights reserved.

Library of Congress Cataloging-in-Publication Record available at https://lccn.loc.gov/2020054045

ISBNs: 978-1-5460-1598-7 (paper over board), 978-1-5460-1605-2 (ebook)

Printed in the United States of America

LSC-C

Printing 3, 2022

CONTENTS

*Whatever you hold in your mind will tend
to occur in your life. If you continue
to believe as you have always believed,
you will continue to act as you have always
acted. If you continue to act as you have
always acted, you will continue to get
what you have always gotten. If you want
different results in your life or your work,
all you have to do is change your mind.*

ANONYMOUS

INTRODUCTION

Are you completely satisfied with every aspect of your life? Or are there areas you would like to change? Are there parts of your life where you feel you need to grow and become stronger? Are there goals you want to reach and dreams you long to fulfill? Is there something you believe you were made to do or be, and you just can't seem to get there? *The key to changing your life is changing your thinking.* As you develop thought patterns (mindsets) that agree with God's Word, everything about your existence will begin to improve. In some cases, your experiences will change, and in other situations, the change in your thinking will cause you to view the same circumstances from a different perspective—and that will change your life. Either way, you win.

Your thinking is more powerful than you may realize. Everything in life begins with a thought, and your thoughts become the mindsets that chart your course in life and ultimately determine your destination. Your mindsets impact everything within you and everything you encounter. Every word you speak and every action you take originates in the mind. Your mindsets form your attitudes; they produce certain opinions and perspectives; they shape your self-image; they affect your relationships; they determine how productive you will be personally and professionally; they heavily influence your priorities; they guide the way you use your time, energy, and financial resources; and they make the difference between success and failure. There is no area of your life that your thinking does not touch. I cannot overemphasize how significant your thoughts are.

Your thinking can work for you or against

you in surprisingly powerful ways. This is because the mind is not simply a function of your human body; it is part of the human soul, along with the emotions and the will (the ability to make choices). The mind is also a spiritual battleground, and the thoughts you think will either help you grow in your relationship with God or hinder you by causing you to think the way your enemy, Satan, wants you to think. It is the ground on which you wage war not only with the enemy over your personal life and your destiny, but also with worldviews and concepts or ideas that threaten to deceive you. It is the battlefield on which you make the decisions that lead to frustration and defeat or the ones that lead to strength, health, love, joy, peace, and abundance.

> *Your thinking can work for you or against you in surprisingly powerful ways.*

Scripture clearly teaches that we become what we think about. Thoughts and mindsets have the ability to make people happy, positive, strong, successful people or frustrated, negative, weak people. Mindsets make the difference between those who reach their goals and live their dreams and those who never seem to be able to do what they really want to do.

Before I continue, I want to state emphatically that I do not believe we can think into existence anything we want. That view of the power of thoughts is a form of humanism, which is an ungodly philosophy. But simply recognizing the fact that thoughts are powerful is not humanistic at all. In fact, it's quite biblical, according to Proverbs 23:7 (NKJV).

The Bible teaches us that our minds must go through a process of renewal in order to experience God's plan for us (Rom. 12:2). His thoughts are above our thoughts (Isa. 55:8–9), so in order to walk with Him and experience His good plans for our lives, we must learn to think as He thinks. Human nature is not bent toward thinking godly thoughts, but we can choose and discipline ourselves to do so.

Few people realize that we have the ability to choose our thoughts and decide what we want to think; most of us passively meditate on whatever comes into our minds without ever realizing that the enemy uses our minds to control us and keep us from fulfilling God's plans and purposes for our lives. It is important to understand that while becoming a Christian immediately affects a person's heart and spirit, it does not suddenly cause a person to think differently. Each person who experiences regeneration through receiving Jesus Christ as Savior and Lord receives a new spirit and a new heart from God. But our natural minds must be renewed, and we must learn to think with the mind of Christ in accordance with God's Word. The intent of a person's heart may be pure while the mind is still confused. The Bible declares that we are to be transformed by the entire renewal of our minds and attitudes (Rom. 12:2). We do this through diligent, thorough study of God's Word and thinking accordingly.

Choosing to think powerfully is not always easy. One of the greatest breakthroughs I have ever experienced took place when I finally realized I had the ability to control my thoughts, and one of the greatest challenges I have ever faced was the challenge to change my thinking once I realized that was possible. You can read more about my journey toward godly thinking in my books *Battlefield of the Mind* and *Power Thoughts*, on which this book is based.

I refer to the twelve chapter titles of this book as "mindsets of the victorious believer."

> *Choosing to think powerfully is not always easy.*

Each chapter addresses a vitally important mindset for a Christian to develop. You have the power to develop them *because you are in Christ*. Apart from Him, we have nothing, we are nothing, and we can do nothing (John

15:5). But in Him, we have everything, we are everything, and we can do everything that is God's will (Phil. 4:13). With His help, powerful, renewed thinking is possible.

You may want to approach the chapters of this book as a twelve-week program by focusing on one each week, or a study over the course of a year by working on one per month. They will take time to become ingrained in your thinking; some will take much longer than a week or a month. I am simply suggesting ways you might approach this book.

As your thinking changes, you may find yourself doing well with a certain thought pattern for a period of time and then feeling you have slipped back into old thinking. That's okay; because you recognized it, you can change it. Changing your thinking is a process that may seem quite challenging at times. They key to it is not to give up when you struggle to align your thoughts with God's Word. Continue to meditate and speak aloud the mindsets of each chapter, and in due time you will see that your thought patterns have truly changed.

The mindsets in this book are based on truths that are realities to us when we are in Christ. There is no true power apart from the power God gives His people, and to really think powerfully, we must think as God teaches us to think. I remind you that changing your thinking will change your life. I am convinced that powerful thinking leads to powerful living, and I believe that as you develop the twelve mindsets addressed in this book, you will begin to live a life that is wonderful beyond your wildest dreams.

Because I am in Christ

I Can Do Everything
I Need to Do in Life

I have strength for all things in Christ Who empowers me [I am ready for anything and equal to anything through Him Who infuses inner strength into me; I am self-sufficient in Christ's sufficiency].

PHILIPPIANS 4:13 AMPC

Do you believe you can do whatever you need to do in life? Or are there certain situations that trigger dread or fear or cause you to say, "I could never do that!" Almost everyone can think of some circumstance that truly seems impossible, something they aren't sure they can handle.

The fact is, while some situations may be undesirable or difficult for you, through Christ you *can* do whatever you need to do in life. I know this because God's Word says that we have the strength to do all things because Christ empowers us to do so (Phil. 4:13). He doesn't say all things will be easy for us, and He doesn't promise we will enjoy every little thing we do, but we can enjoy life in the midst of every situation we face. In Him, we have the strength to do everything we need to do because He Himself empowers us and gives us the sufficiency we need.

WITH GOD'S HELP

Philippians 4:13 does not say we can do anything we want to do because we are strong enough, smart enough, or diligent enough. We can do what we need to do, meaning anything God wants us to do, but not just anything we decide we want to do. The key to being able to do what we need to do is realizing that we cannot do it alone; we can only do it in Christ. For some reason, we often think we have to do whatever we need to do through our human strength and abilities. We tend to forget that the power of Christ works through us, so we are defeated before we even begin. We are partners with God; we cannot do His part and He will not do our part. He will guide and help us in all we need to do, but He wants us to respond to His direction and leading, relying completely on Him every step of the way.

You may be tempted at times to think, *This is too hard. I just can't do this. It's too much for me.* But as a believer in Jesus Christ, you are full of God's Spirit, and nothing is too difficult for you if God is leading you to do it. He will not call you to do anything that He will not enable and empower you to do.

> *God will not call you to do anything that He will not enable and empower you to do.*

Difficult situations arise in everyone's life, and although God never authors our troubles, He does use them for our spiritual growth. Our attitude toward life's difficulties is actually more important than the challenges themselves, and it is a vital part of getting through them successfully. If you will develop an increasingly positive, faith-filled attitude, you will find that your trials are not as bad as you think and that, in fact, they can be steppingstones to your greatest victories.

God has given you the gifts, talents, abilities, and grace you need to do His will. God's grace is His power at work on your behalf. He will not only give you grace, but He promises grace and more grace (James 4:6). He never runs out of power—and that power is available to you through Christ. If you don't think thoughts that affirm and remind you that God's power is working through you, the enemy can defeat you with thoughts of inadequacy. But if you make up your mind that you can do what you need to do, you'll find yourself able to do it—not in your own strength, but in the strength that God gives you.

THINK POWERFULLY, SPEAK POWERFULLY

Jesus says, "The mouth speaks what the heart is full of" (Luke 6:45). We can learn a lot about ourselves by listening to what we say. Let me ask you: Do your thoughts and words reflect your complete dependence on God, realizing that His abilities—not your own—empower you to do anything you need to do in life? At times, I have had to examine my own thoughts and words and ask myself if I portrayed a person who had faith in God, and I encourage you to do the same. I didn't like all of my answers, but the exercise in self-examination did open my eyes to see that I needed to make some changes.

Realizing we are wrong in an area is never a problem. The problem comes when we refuse to face truth and make the changes God is leading us to make. As you ask yourself whether or not you come across as a person of great faith in God, I encourage you to be willing to face anything He wants to show you and ask Him to change you. If you are trusting in your own strength, begin to trust Him instead. If you are becoming frustrated trying to do things out of your own human abilities, tell God you want Him to work through you, and let His sufficiency be your sufficiency.

When challenges arise, I encourage you to develop a habit of saying immediately, "I can do whatever I need to do through Christ, who is my strength." Words are containers for power, and speaking words that agree with God's Word will help you do what God wants you to do. Don't fill your containers

> *I can do whatever I need to do through Christ, who is my strength.*

(words) with things that *dis*able you but with things that *en*able you.

As you meditate on this truth that through Christ you can do whatever you need to do, you will find that you are not as easily overwhelmed by situations that once discouraged you. Each time you roll that thought over in your mind or speak it, you are developing a healthy mind-set that empowers you to be victorious in any situation.

NO MORE EXCUSES

One reason many people do not enjoy their lives, miss out on some of the blessings God wants to give them, or feel bad about themselves is that they do not truly believe they can do whatever they need to do, so they quit when they meet challenges. They never taste the joy of a goal accomplished or a desire fulfilled because they do not press past the difficulties that arise.

Everyone has their go-to excuses. When

something hard or undesirable happens and challenges us or gives us more than we want to deal with, we think or say:

- "That is just too hard."
- "I don't have enough time."
- "I hadn't planned on this today."
- "I don't have the money."
- "I don't have anyone to help me."
- "I can't see how that would ever work."
- "I just don't feel like it."
- "I have too many personal problems and too much going on in my life right now."
- "I don't know how to do that."
- "I have never done this. I don't even know anybody who's ever done this."
- "I'm afraid."

Many of these thoughts are based on emotions (the way you feel about a situation). Let me encourage you not to think or speak out of your emotions; how you feel does not always agree with God's Word. That is why it is important to realize that even though you feel overwhelmed, you should still say, "Because I am in Christ, I can do everything I need to do in life."

I hope you will begin right now to stop looking at all your weaknesses and insufficiencies, allowing them to tell you what you can and cannot do, because God's strength is made perfect in your weakness (2 Cor. 12:9). Through human weakness and inability, He displays His strength. He deliberately chooses people who absolutely cannot do what He is asking them to do unless they allow Him to do it through them. With God, you don't need ability; you simply need availability and a can-do attitude.

> *With God, you don't need ability; you simply need availability and a can-do attitude.*

If you will exchange "I can't" excuses for "I can" thoughts and begin to say, "I can do whatever I need to do in life because God strengthens me. I am strong in the

Lord and in the power of His might, and whatever He asks me to do, I can do," remarkable changes will begin to happen and you will have more zeal and enthusiasm as you face each day.

YOU'RE MORE THAN
A CONQUEROR

Romans 8:37 teaches us how to think about the challenges we face: "In all these things we are more than conquerors through him who loved us."

I believe that being "more than a conqueror" means having such confidence in God that no matter what we face, we know that through Him we can overcome it. We know before we ever encounter a problem that we will gain victory over it. We believe that, with His help, we can do whatever we need to do. Therefore, we don't dread anything; we don't fear the unknown; we don't live in anxiety about what will happen in any situation. It doesn't really matter what the challenge is; we know we can handle it through Christ. Defeat is not an option.

Thinking about negative circumstances too long will empower those circumstances to overwhelm us. No wonder the Bible says we should look away from things that distract us and instead fix our eyes on Jesus, who is "the Leader and the Source of our faith" and who brings our faith to maturity (Hebrews 12:2 AMPC). We need to remember at all times that *He* is the one who empowers us to do all things, and look to Him regularly throughout each day.

If you will begin to think every day, *I can handle whatever life hands me. I can do whatever I need to do in life. I am more than a conqueror. I am equal to anything through Him who infuses inner strength into me*, even before you get out of bed in the mornings—just let it roll over and over in your mind—your confidence will skyrocket, and you will find that indeed, in Him, you can do whatever you need to do in life.

THINK, THEN ACT

1. What do you need to begin to believe you can do with God's help? What steps will you take to do it?

....

....

2. What will you begin to think and say to reflect your confidence in God's ability to help you do whatever you need to do?

....

....

3. In what specific situation do you need to believe you are more than a conqueror? How can you act on that belief?

....

....

Because I am in Christ

I Am Loved Unconditionally

Even as [in His love] He chose us [actually picked us out for Himself as His own] in Christ before the foundation of the world, that we should be holy (consecrated and set apart for Him) and blameless in His sight, even above reproach, before Him in love.

EPHESIANS 1:4 AMPC

What's wrong with me?"

If you are like most people, you have asked yourself this question many times. It's a common query that the enemy plants in people's minds, and I asked it for many years. It is designed to make you feel that you are not what you need to be and to prevent you from enjoying yourself and your life.

The enemy wants you to ask what's wrong with you so you will become self-focused by trying to figure out what's wrong with you. God does not want you to be tormented by this question. He wants you to know how much He loves you. When you truly believe God loves and accepts you unconditionally, the enemy will no longer be able to make you feel bad about yourself. You might feel bad about something you have done wrong, but you won't feel bad about yourself if you realize that God never stops loving you for even one second.

Not only does God love you, but He chooses to view you as right with Him, accepted and blameless (2 Cor. 5:21). This comes through faith in Jesus Christ as your Savior and Lord. Because this is true, you can accurately say, "I am the righteousness of God in Christ. I am chosen in Christ, and in Him I am blameless before God." This is your inherited position with God through faith in Jesus, not through works you view as "right" or "wrong."

While God does want you to learn proper behavior, He accepts and loves you first, before you ever do anything that pleases Him. Once you are rooted and grounded in His unconditional love, then He begins transforming your character into the image of His Son. If you want your behavior to improve, then your knowledge of the unconditional love of God must be the foundation for the "new you." The more you experience His love, the more you will desire to do what pleases Him.

RELATIONSHIP, NOT RELIGION

Jesus didn't die so we could be religious; Jesus died so we could have deep, intimate, personal relationship with God through Him. Legalistic religion offers us rules and regulations to follow in order to be close to God. But relationship allows us to be close to Him because He has chosen us as His beloved children. There is nothing we can do to earn or merit His love. He simply *is* love (1 John 4:8), and He loves us because of who He is, not because of what we do or don't do.

We will not draw near to God if we are afraid He is displeased with us. That's why it is vital that we know the difference between our "who" and our "do"—that we learn how to separate *who* we are in Christ and how important we are to God from *what* we do, whether we feel it's good or bad. Only when we can separate the two will we begin to be confident that we are loved unconditionally. When we sin, we should admit it and repent, but God still views us through Christ, and we are still in right standing with Him.

> *Relationship allows us to be close to God because He has chosen us as His beloved children.*

Too often, the enemy succeeds in deceiving

us into thinking that our acceptance is based on our performance. This is totally unscriptural. God loves and accepts us completely. We are made right with Him because we place our faith in Jesus Christ and the work He accomplished for us on the cross. He paid for our sins and misdeeds. He absolved us from guilt and reconciled us to God. Now, when we stand before God, we have "rightness," not "wrongness." And we have it because He gave it as a gift, not because we have earned it.

I once saw a bumper sticker that said, "I owe, I owe, so off to work I go." I immediately realized that I had lived my spiritual life with that mentality for years. I felt that I owed God something for all the wrong I had done, and I tried every day to do good works to make up for my mistakes. I wanted Him to bless me, but felt I needed to earn His blessings. I finally learned that we cannot pay for God's gifts; otherwise, they are not gifts at all.

God sees our hearts, and His dealings with us

are based on the kind of heart we have toward Him. I don't do everything right, but I do love God very much, and I want His will in my life. I am very sorry for my sins, and it grieves me when I know I have disappointed Him. I am sure that, since you are reading this book, the attitude of your heart is the same as mine. Per-

> *Knowing that God loves you unconditionally releases you from negative emotions.*

haps like I was, you have been tormented for years wondering what is wrong with you. Knowing that God loves you unconditionally releases you from those negative emotions and allows you to enjoy yourself while you are changing and growing in Him.

JESUS PAID THE HIGHEST PRICE

The fact that God sent His only beloved Son to die a painful death in our place assigns value to us and lets us know He loves us immensely. We are bought with a price, the highest, most precious price—the blood of Jesus (1 Pet. 1:18–19). He paid for our misdeeds, secured our justification, balanced our accounts with God, and absolved us from all guilt (Rom. 4:25).

At the cross, Jesus stood in our place, taking what we deserved (punishment as sinners) and freely giving us what He deserves (every kind of blessing). His sacrifice immediately transferred us, through faith, from a state of being wrong to a state of being viewed by God as right through faith in Jesus. His death and resurrection transferred us out of the misery and torment of the enemy's kingdom into the unspeakable blessings of God's kingdom, to live as His beloved children (1 Pet. 2:9; Col. 1:13). The grace of God purchased our freedom, and faith is the hand that reaches out and receives it.

Nothing ever done on Earth could even come close to the awesome gift Jesus gave us on the cross. God's justice required that our sins be paid for and Jesus paid everything we could ever owe.

PERFORMANCE CANCELED

Our experiences in the world have told us that we cannot be accepted apart from "performing" well in life and that our performances determine how much acceptance we receive. We have been deceived into believing that what we do is more important than who we are. This leaves us constantly working to prove to ourselves and others that what we do determines our value.

As long as we think God's love is conditional, we will keep trying to earn it by attempting to prove that we are worth loving. Then, when we make mistakes, we feel we are no longer valuable and therefore do not deserve love. We suffer the guilt, shame, and condemnation of believing we are not lovable and should be rejected. We keep trying harder and harder until sometimes we are exhausted mentally, emotionally, spiritually, and even physically. We try to put up a good front, but inside we are weary and often very afraid.

Once we believe God's love is based on who He is and what Jesus has done for us on the cross—not on what we do—the struggle is over. We can cancel our "performance" and serve God because we *know* that He does love us and we do not need to "get" Him to love us. We already know we have His love and that under no condition will He ever stop loving us (Rom. 8:38–39). We no longer have to live in fear of His rejecting us because of our mistakes. When we do something that does not please God, all we need to do is repent, receive His forgiveness,

> *We have God's love, and under no condition will He ever stop loving us.*

and refuse the guilt that comes with sin. That guilt no longer applies to us once sin is forgiven and removed.

God is displeased when we sin (this is our "do," not our "who"), but He *always* loves us.

He loves us enough to correct us and continue working with us to bring us into more godly behavior (Heb. 12:10). We are destined to be molded into the image of Jesus Christ (Rom. 8:29), and I am grateful that He has sent His Holy Spirit to convict us of sin and to work His holiness in and through us. This is a work of God's grace, and it takes place little by little as we study God's Word (2 Cor. 3:18).

An important verse to understand as we learn to believe we are loved and in right standing with God is 2 Corinthians 5:21: "God made him who had no sin to be sin for us, so that in him we might become the righteousness of God." Knowing we are loved and accepted even in our imperfections is such a relief! Serving God from a sense of desire rather than from a feeling of obligation is incredibly liberating and brings great peace and joy to our lives. The Bible says that we love Him because He first loved us (1 John 4:19). Being assured of God's unconditional love gives us confidence and boldness, and it makes us more than conquerors in every situation (Rom. 8:37).

Our confidence should not be in anything or anyone but Jesus. We can count on Him to always be faithful and do what He says He will do—and He says He will always love us. He says we are righteous in His sight, and we need to choose simply to believe it.

No matter what other people may say, God delights in telling you

> *We are more than conquerors in every situation.*

in His Word who you are in Him—loved, valuable, precious, talented, gifted, capable, powerful, wise, and redeemed. He has a good plan for you. Get excited about your life. You are created in God's image, you are amazing, and you are loved unconditionally.

THINK, THEN ACT

1. In your own words, how do you believe God feels about you? Now say, "God loves me unconditionally!"

2. List five positive things about yourself. You may find this difficult if you have never done it, but be bold.

3. Draw a line down the center of a piece of paper. On one side of the line, write "Who," and on the other side, write "Do." Under "Who," list who you are according to God's Word, and under "Do" list things you do right and things you do wrong. This will help you separate who you are from what you do. Now cross out the "Do" section, because it has nothing to do with God's love for you. Look only at who you are in Him!

Because I am in Christ

I Will Not Live in Fear

For the Spirit God gave us does not make us timid, but gives us power, love and self-discipline.

2 Timothy 1:7

Until the power of fear is broken in our lives, we are not free to do what is in our hearts or to follow God. To fulfill His good plan for our lives and to enjoy all the blessings He wants to give us, we simply must refuse to allow fear to control us. Fear brings torment, and when it rules our lives, we cannot enjoy anything we do. But when we are free from fear, we can live joyful lives of peace, satisfaction, and blessing.

HOW FEAR OPERATES

Fear can absolutely paralyze us, which is why Satan uses it to steal from us in many ways. For example, the fear that we will not be accepted as we are causes us to develop phony personalities that stifle our true selves and hide who God has made us to be. The fear of failure prevents us from trying new things or reaching beyond our comfort zones. The fear of the future can cause us not to enjoy the present.

I believe fear is the devil's tool to keep us unhappy, frustrated, and out of God's will. It drains our courage, gives us a negative viewpoint, and prevents us from making progress. Destinies are destroyed because of fear—fear of pain, fear of discomfort, fear of lack, fear of sacrifice, fear that life is going to be too hard, fear of losing friends, fear of being alone, fear of losing our reputation, fear that no one will understand us, fear that we are missing God, and on and on.

Fear is the enemy's perversion of faith. He says, "Believe what I'm telling you. What you are trying to do is not going to work. Your prayers aren't any good. You aren't in right standing with God. You are a failure." Fear always tells you what you're not, what you don't have, what you can't do, and what you never will be. But God's Word tells you who you are, what you have, what you can do, and who you can be in Him. The enemy will try to use fear to control your life, but you can refuse to allow it to do so.

> *God's Word tells you who you are, what you have, what you can do, and who you can be in Him.*

You can be bold, courageous, and adventurous. The only way to defeat fear is to confront it and not let it stop you from doing what you know you should do, even if you have to "do it afraid."

BOREDOM

God created you for the exhilaration of a life that requires you to take bold steps of faith and see Him come through for you. Many people are unsatisfied with their lives simply because they won't step out into the new things they desire to do. They want to feel secure, but security does not always make room for life's great joys and adventures.

Boredom is often the result of sameness. I encourage you to include more variety in your life. Try new things; when you start feeling that life is getting stale and tasteless add a little spice by doing something different. Don't let fear keep you from the vibrant life God has for you or destroy your destiny. Start thinking and saying, "I will not live in fear." You may feel afraid at times, but you can choose to push through fear and do what you want to do anyway. You may have to do it afraid, but you can still do it. If you struggle in this area, I encourage you to read my book *Do It Afraid*.

IT WON'T GO AWAY

We must learn how to deal with fear effectively *before* it paralyzes us. This is because it will never completely go away. Feeling fear is part of being alive. We may feel fearful when we are doing something we have never done, or when obstacles seem insurmountable, or when we don't have the natural help we feel we need. None of this means we are cowards; it means we are human. We can only be cowardly when we allow fear to dictate our actions or decisions instead of following our hearts and doing what we know is right for us. Feeling fear is simply the *temptation* to run away from what we should confront; it does not mean we let fearful feelings get the best of us and make decisions for us.

When God said to various people in the Bible, "Fear not," He was basically telling them, "Fear *will* come after you. You are going to have to deal with it." No matter what you feel like, just keep going forward and you will arrive at your desired destination. I am not suggesting doing foolish things, but if you are fully assured that God is directing you, then press forward no matter what you feel like or what people say. I often say, "Courage is not the absence of fear; it is progress in its presence."

It's okay to feel fear; it's not okay to act on fearful feelings. Fear does not mean to shake or quake or have a dry mouth or weak knees. I have read many definitions of the word *fear*, and I like to say that *fear* simply means "to take flight" or "to run away from." It tempts us to flee what God wants us to confront. Fear is not a feeling; fear is an evil spirit that produces a feeling. When we say, "I will not bow down to fear," what we mean is "I will not shrink back in fear." Fear causes us to cower and withdraw. It causes us to have little faith instead of big faith, and if we entertain it long enough, we'll end up with no faith at all.

> *Courage is not the absence of fear; it is progress in its presence.*

The only acceptable attitude for a Christian to have toward fear is "I will not fear." God knows that a person's first impulse when feeling fear is to begin to shrink back. This is why He says, "Do not fear," meaning that no matter how you feel, keep putting one foot in front of the other and doing what you believe He has told you to do because that is the only way to defeat fear and make progress.

PRAY AND SAY

I spent many years as a very fearful person, though my personality was strong and I seemed quite bold. To help me break free from fear, God taught me to use what I call the "power twins" to help me defeat it: I pray and I say. When I feel fear, I begin to pray and ask for God's help, and I say, "I will not fear!" I've also learned to say, "Fear will always present itself to me, but I will ignore it and keep going forward."

I started overcoming fear by praying and by

thinking and saying, "I will not live in fear." Remember, fear means "to take flight or run away from something." I learned that I had to stop running and stand still long enough to see what God would do for me if I let my faith in Him be larger than my fears. I finally realized that each time God was leading me into a new area that would eventually be better for me, the enemy launched an attack of fear against me.

Fear is the enemy's favorite weapon, and he uses it masterfully against us until we realize that in Christ, we have the power to move beyond fear and keep making progress. You can also use the power twins—I pray and I say—as soon as you feel fearful about anything. They will keep fear from controlling you. You may still feel fear, but you can move beyond it by realizing that it is merely the enemy's attempt to prevent you from enjoying life or making any kind of progress. Do what you

> *Do what you believe you are supposed to do even if you have to "do it afraid."*

believe you are supposed to do even if you have to "do it afraid."

BE FILLED WITH FAITH

Fear is the opposite of faith. The enemy tries to manipulate us through fear, while God wants to bless us through faith. Fear is the enemy's counterfeit of faith. In other words, we can know and do God's will through placing our faith in Him, and we can cooperate with the enemy's desires through fear.

When fear knocks on the door of our lives, if it finds us full of faith, it cannot enter. I strongly urge you to meditate on and confess that you are filled with faith. I say it like this: "I am a woman of faith. I think faith, talk faith, and walk in faith." I also choose portions of Scripture about faith and meditate on them. Fear weakens us in every way, but faith adds courage, boldness, confidence, and energy to our lives.

When Satan comes to attack you with fear,

make sure you are filled with faith so there will be no place of entrance for him. Fear and faith cannot coexist; where you have one, you will not have the other. God's Word builds faith in your heart, so study it and meditate on it—and you'll keep fear out of your life.

GOD IS WITH YOU

To overcome fear, we must believe that God is with us (Josh. 1:9; Isa. 41:10). This is the key to being able to obey His often-repeated instruction in Scripture "Do not fear." If we are confident that God is with us, we will not be afraid.

We can easily feel afraid if we think about the future and the things that are unknown to us. We can look at it two ways. Either we can be negative and fearful, or we can be excited about being part of God's mystery, knowing that He knows exactly what's going to happen and is right there with us, helping us and directing us.

God is never surprised by anything. He

knows everything before it happens, and He has already planned our deliverance, so all we need to do is simply take one step at a time. We don't need to worry about the next step, because God will be there to guide us when the time comes.

God is with us at all times, under all circumstances. This powerful truth can absolutely demolish fear in our lives. We don't have to see or feel Him in order to believe He is near. Faith is a matter of the heart, not the natural senses.

> *God knows exactly what's going to happen and is right there with us, helping us and directing us.*

Let me encourage you to believe that God is with you and to begin living free from fear. The more aware you are of God's presence, the more confident you will be. You only have one life to live, so live it boldly and never let fear steal God's best for you!

THINK, THEN ACT

1. Take a moment to think about how your life would be if you were free from all fear. How would a fear-free life differ from the life you have today?

....

....

2. In what ways is fear causing you to live a safe but boring life? What will you do to break free from it and do something you've always wanted to do even though it may be outside your comfort zone?

....

....

3. What can you do to keep fear from controlling you by influencing your decisions?

....

....

Because I am in Christ

I Am Difficult to Offend

Great peace have they who love Your law; nothing shall offend them or make them stumble.

PSALM 119:165 AMPC

People who want to live powerful lives must become experts at forgiving those who offend and hurt them. Developing the mindset that you are difficult to offend will make your life much more pleasant. People are everywhere, and you never know what they might say or do. Refusing to forgive someone gives that person control over your life, and why would anyone want to do that? Being hurt and offended does not change the people; it only changes you. It makes you miserable and steals your peace and joy, so why not prepare yourself mentally *not* to fall into Satan's trap? Being offended will not change the person who hurt you, but it will change you. It will make you bitter, withdrawn, and often revengeful, and it will focus your thoughts on things that do not bear good fruit in your life.

OPPORTUNITIES FOR OFFENSE ABOUND

As long as we are around people, we will have opportunities to be offended. The temptation to become hurt, angry, or offended comes just as surely as any other temptation comes. Praying that temptation won't present itself to us does no good, but we can choose to take it or leave it when we face it. Allowing ourselves to become offended is very serious and has devastating consequences. Satan will not stop tempting us to be offended, but the Holy Spirit gives us the power to resist him.

One of the signs of the last days prior to Jesus' return is that offense will increase.

> And then many will be offended and repelled and will begin to distrust and desert [Him Whom they ought to trust and obey] and will stumble and fall away and betray one another and pursue one another with hatred.
>
> Matthew 24:10 AMPC

Rudeness, quick tempers, and holding grudges seem to be common today. Sometimes I think more people in the world are angry and offended than those who are not. People are playing right into the devil's hands when they allow negative and poisonous emotions to rule them. I hope you will think and say often, "In Christ, I am difficult to offend."

LET GOD DO IT

One reason we find forgiving others difficult when we are offended is that we have heard and told ourselves repeatedly that forgiving is hard to do. We have set our minds to fail at one of God's most important commands—to forgive and pray for our enemies and those who hurt and abuse us (Luke 6:35–36). We meditate too much on what the offensive person has done to us and not enough on the forgiveness God has extended to us.

While praying for our enemies and blessing those who curse us may seem difficult, we can do it if we set our minds to it. God never tells us to do anything that is not good for us, and never requires anything we cannot do. I believe that forgiving those who hurt and offend us is one of the most spiritually powerful things we can do, and God gives us the strength to do it (Phil. 4:13). The Bible says we are to "overcome evil with good" (Rom. 12:21).

BELIEVE THE BEST

Believing the best of people helps greatly in the process of forgiving people who hurt or offend us. As human beings, we tend to be suspicious of others, and we often get hurt due to our own imaginations. It is possible to believe someone wounded us intentionally when the truth is that they were not even aware they did anything at all and would be grieved to know that they hurt us. God calls us to love others, and love always believes the best (1 Cor. 13:7).

> God calls us to love others, and love always believes the best.

I encourage you to believe the best about others. Resist the temptation to question their motives or to think they hurt you deliberately. Believing the best about people will keep offense and bitterness out of your life and help you stay peaceful and joyful.

TIRED, TOUCHY, AND OVERSENSITIVE

Sometimes we are more prone to be hurt or offended than at other times. Years of experience have taught me that when I am excessively tired, I am touchier and more apt to get my feelings hurt than when I am rested. I have learned to avoid conversations that could be tense when I know I am tired. I have also learned to wait to bring up subjects that might be tense for Dave when he is tired. I encourage husbands and wives to learn to relate to each other in ways that minimize the potential for offense, just as Dave and I have learned to do.

I have also discovered I can be more easily offended than I typically am when I have been working too long without a break. I might not be physically tired, but I may be mentally fatigued and need some creativity or diversity. Understanding these dynamics about myself has helped me avoid offense. I can say to myself,

"I am tired and therefore touchy, so I need to shake this off and not get upset over something I wouldn't normally get upset about."

When we are tempted to sin by being offended, we may need to give ourselves verbal instructions such as, "I know I am tired and frustrated, but I am not going to sin. I will not open a door to the enemy in my life by being offended. I am going to obey God and forgive this person, and not harbor hurt and offense in my heart."

Let me encourage you to instruct yourself as often as needed in order to figure out when you are most likely to be easily offended. As I mentioned, I am more sensitive to offense when I am tired or under stress, and I believe most of us are that way. For some women, "that time of the month" is when they are extremely sensitive or prone to outbursts. For others, going through the change of life is a time when emotions can fluctuate greatly. Get to know yourself and be aware when circumstances that make you touchy arise. During those times, be diligent to refuse to be offended.

IT'S A CHOICE

Deciding not to be offended does not always change how we feel about the way someone has treated us. One of our biggest problems is that we usually allow our feelings to direct our choices and never get around to making the decisions we need to make. However, our feelings will eventually catch up with our decisions, so we need to be responsible to make godly decisions and let the feelings follow. Becoming established in the thought *In Christ, I am difficult to offend* can prepare you ahead of time for any offense you may face. It will set you up to forgive and release the offender, which will keep you out of the snare of unforgiveness.

A wise person refuses to live with hurt feelings or offense in his or her heart. Life is too short to waste one day being angry, bitter, and resentful. Jesus forgives all our sins and gives us the ability to forgive those who sin against us. Anything God gives us, such as forgiveness and mercy, He expects us to extend it to others. When we are offended, we need to quickly call to mind the fact that God has freely and fully forgiven us, so we should freely and fully forgive others.

> *Anything God gives us, He expects us to extend it to others.*

THE BENEFITS OF FORGIVENESS

Mark 11:22–26 clearly teaches us that unforgiveness hinders our faith from working, so we can conclude in contrast that forgiveness enables faith to work for us. Our heavenly Father can't forgive our sins if we don't forgive other people (Matthew 6:14–15). But faith that works is not the only benefit of forgiveness. In addition, we're happier and we feel better physically when we're not filled with the poison of unforgiveness. Serious diseases can develop as a result of the stress and pressure that result from bitterness, resentment, and unforgiveness.

Also, our fellowship with God flows freely when we're willing to forgive, but unforgiveness serves as a major block to communion with Him. Furthermore, I believe it is difficult to love people while harboring anger toward others. Any kind of bitterness in our hearts seeps out in all of our attitudes and relationships, but forgiving our enemies sets us free to move on with our lives.

Finally, forgiveness keeps Satan from gaining an advantage over us (2 Cor. 2:10–11). Ephesians 4:26–27 tells us not to let the sun go down on our anger or give the devil any opportunity. Remember that the enemy must have a foothold before he can get a stronghold. Do not help Satan torture you through feelings of offense. Be quick to forgive when you are offended.

A KEY ISSUE FOR DESPERATE TIMES

I cannot stress enough how important it is to become difficult to offend. Satan desperately tries to prevent us from making spiritual progress. If he can keep us focused on who we are angry with and what they did to offend us, then we cannot focus on God's Word and His plan for us, and we will not grow spiritually.

Most of us sense that we are living in desperate times among desperate people, and we should be more careful than ever before not to let our emotions take the lead in our lives. Instead of being quick to anger or offense, we must take the Bible's advice and be wise as serpents and gentle as doves (Matt. 10:16). In other words, we should be spiritually mature, patient, kind, and gentle with others and wise enough not to allow them to offend us. We cannot control what people do to us, but in Christ we can control the way we respond to them.

The world seems to be growing darker and

darker. Everywhere we look, we hear about people whose anger leads them to do drastic, even tragic, things. We want to represent God and express His love in these difficult days, and to do so, we will have to guard our hearts diligently against offense and anger. Building the mindset that you are not easy to offend will be very helpful to you and all those you love.

THINK, THEN ACT

1. In what areas do you frequently fall into the enemy's trap of being offended? How can you think powerfully about those things so you can prepare yourself ahead of time for victory?

....

....

2. List several ways you can benefit from forgiving someone. Now, think about who has offended you and take the important step of forgiving them.

....

....

3. In your own words, why is it important to become a person who is difficult to offend?

....

....

Because I am in Christ

I Love People and Enjoy Helping Them

A new command I give you: Love one another. As I have loved you, so you must love one another.

JOHN 13:34

If I could only preach one message, it would probably be this: Take your mind off of yourself and spend your life trying to do as much as possible for others. From start to finish, God's Word encourages and challenges us to love other people. To love others is the "new commandment" Jesus gives us in John 13:34 and the example He set for us throughout His earthly life and ministry. If we want to be like Jesus, we need to love others with the same kind of gracious, forgiving, generous, unconditional love He extends to us.

Nothing has changed my life more dramatically than learning how to love people and treat them well. If you only incorporate one powerful mindset to act on from this book, I urge you to make it this one: *Because I am in Christ, I love people and enjoy helping them.*

LOVE = ACTION

Real love is much more than gooey emotions and goose bumps. It has to do with the choices we make about the way we treat people. Real love is not theory or talk; it is action. It is a decision concerning the way we behave in our relationships with others. Real love goes beyond talk or theory and meets

> *Real love goes beyond talk or theory and meets needs even when meeting them requires sacrifice.*

needs even when meeting them requires sacrifice. First John 3:18 says: "Let us not love with
words or speech but with actions and in truth."

Let me ask you: Would you commit before
God, sincerely in your heart, to do at least one
thing for somebody else every day? This may
sound simple, but to act on this commitment,
you will have to think about it and do it on
purpose. You may even have to move beyond
the normal group of people in your life and do
things for people to whom you would not normally reach out, including strangers. Many people in the world have never, ever had anyone do
anything nice for them, and they are desperate
for some words or acts of love.

When love is the theme of your life, you will
have a life worth living. If you truly desire to
excel in walking in love, the first step to take is
to fill your mind with kind, loving, unselfish,
generous thoughts. Remember, it is impossible
to change your behavior unless you change your
mind. Start thinking loving, generous thoughts

today, and start asking God to show you who you can bless and what you can do for them—and you'll soon have a life filled with love and happiness.

WHAT ABOUT ME?

Caring about other people is the greatest thing we can ever do because, as human beings, we are selfish and our thoughts tend to be focused on ourselves. Whether we ever speak these words or not, we constantly ask, "What about me? What about me? What about me?" This is not the way God wants us to live.

Jesus tells us plainly what we need to do if we want to follow Him: "Whoever wants to be my disciple must deny themselves and take up their cross and follow me" (Mark 8:34). The "cross" we are to carry is simply one of unselfishness.

Most of us concentrate on what we can *get* in life, but we need to concentrate on what we can *give*. Instead of thinking about what other people should do for us, we should think aggressively about what we can do for others and then trust God to meet our needs and fulfill our desires.

Please notice that I say we need to think *aggressively* about what we can do for others. Galatians 6:10 encourages us to "*be mindful* to be a blessing" (AMPC, emphasis mine). To "be mindful" means to be intentional, to be purposeful and deliberate. God wants us to think on purpose and to deliberately be a blessing to others.

> *God wants us to think on purpose and to deliberately be a blessing to others.*

I encourage you to begin to think on purpose about how you can be a blessing to the people around you. It does not have to cost money, although at times it may; it does not always have to take much time; and it does not have to take lots of energy. Blessing people can be quick and easy, but it won't just happen. You have to do it intentionally. As you use what you have in the service of God and others, your own needs will always be met.

BE A BLESSING DISPENSER

God puts His love in our hearts when we accept Jesus as our Savior, but that love needs to flow *through* us in order for it to help anyone else. In Genesis 12:2, God said He would bless Abraham and make him a person who dispensed blessings everywhere he went. This story reminds me of a bottle of hand lotion with a pump on it. When I press the pump, it dispenses lotion. That's the way I want to be with blessings. When people come near me, I want to dispense something good, something that will benefit them.

I encourage you to use what you have to meet needs for other people and to have what I call "prosperity with a purpose." Don't pray to be prosperous so you can have more and more for yourself, but make certain you use a good portion of what you have to bless others. I am not talking about only putting money into an offering at church on Sundays. I am talking about doing things for people in your daily life—people you work with, people in your family, people you like and people you may not particularly like, people you know and people you don't know, those you think deserve it as well as those you don't think deserve it. This is an exciting way to live, and it will bless you just as it blesses others.

You never know what God has in store when He puts something on your heart to do for someone else—even when it may not make sense to you or when it seems silly or embarrassing. If He asks you to do or give something, do it. I assure you, He always knows what He is doing, so even when you don't understand, go ahead and obey.

I encourage you to spend some time each morning thinking about what you can do for someone else that day. Lie in your bed before you get up and pray, "God, who can I bless today?" In the evening take a "blessing inventory" by asking, "What did I do today to make someone else's life better?" As I started learning to bless others, I found that I often made plans in the morning to bless people later that day, but then became busy and did not follow through. Taking the evening inventory really helped me because I did not want to have to answer, "Nothing—I did nothing to improve someone else's life today."

Decide to use the blessings in your life to be a blessing to others everywhere you go. You can do this in big ways, such as meeting a great financial need, or in small ways, such as simply being friendly. There are countless ways to be a blessing if you think about it

> *Decide to use the blessings in your life to be a blessing to others everywhere you go.*

creatively and ask God to help you. The important thing is to simply do it.

A WONDERFUL LIFE

I once thought being happy meant having
everything I wanted, but I have now learned
that we do not even know what happiness is
until we forget about ourselves, start focusing on others, and become generous givers. In
order to be generous, we have to do more than
simply plunk some change in a charity bucket
during the holidays or give to the church once
a week.

Actually, I think learning to give in church
should simply be practice for the way we live
our everyday lives. I do not want to merely give
offerings; I want to *be*
a giver. I want to offer
myself every day to
be used for whatever
God chooses. For this

> *I want to offer myself every day to be used for whatever God chooses.*

change to take place in my life, I had to change my thinking. I had to think and say thousands of times, "I love people and I enjoy helping them." This mindset will be life-changing for you if you put it to work in your life.

As you become a generous giver, you will be amazed at how happy you will be and how much you will enjoy life. In contrast, stingy people are unhappy. They do only what they have to do, they look out only for themselves, they don't like to share, and they only give when they feel they must—and then, they often do so reluctantly or grudgingly. These attitudes and actions run contrary to the way God wants us to live, because they do not result in blessings for anyone and will actually drain the life out of a person (Prov. 1:19).

God Himself is a giver (Eph. 3:20–21). If we want to be like He is, we need to always go the extra mile, always do more than we have to, always give more than enough, and always be generous.

HOW GENEROUS ARE YOU?

I want to close this chapter with several questions to help you evaluate your level of generosity so that, if needed, you can grow in it.

- How well do you tip? If you were a server, would you want to wait on yourself, based on the way you tip?
- What kinds of gifts do you give? Do you give the cheapest things you can find? Do you buy things just to meet an obligation, or do you sincerely look for what you believe the recipient would enjoy?
- Do you freely and frequently encourage and compliment other people?
- Are you willing to share what you have?
- Do you hoard possessions, or do you give away what you're not using?
- When you have opportunities to give to those less fortunate, do you give as much as you can or as little as you can?

As you develop the mindset that you love people and enjoy helping them, you will become an increasingly generous person who shows God's love by helping people in every way possible and experiences the blessings of truly loving others.

THINK, THEN ACT

1. What practical steps will you take to put love into action today?

....

....

2. Who will you bless this week, and how will you do it?

....

....

3. In what specific ways can you become a more generous person?

....

....

Because I am in Christ

I Trust God Completely and Have No Need to Worry

Trust in the Lord with all your heart and lean not on your own understanding.

Have you noticed how absolutely powerless you feel when you worry or feel anxious and troubled? This is because worry is completely useless. It is a waste of time and energy because it never changes our circumstances. Worry does, however, change us. It can make us grouchy or despondent, and it can even make us sick. A medical researcher once told me that 87 percent of all illness is connected to wrong thought patterns. Worry would certainly fall under the heading of "negative thinking," and negative thoughts actually release chemicals from the brain that affect us adversely. In her popular book *Who Switched Off My Brain?* Dr. Caroline Leaf states that we think thirty thousand thoughts per day, and through an uncontrolled thought life, we create conditions that are favorable for illness. We make ourselves sick!

Worry keeps us from living in faith and steals our peace, while offering nothing productive. Despite the fact that worrying does us no good and is actually detrimental to our well-being, it plagues multitudes of people, maybe even you. It's human nature to be concerned about bad situations, but if we're not careful, concern can easily become worry or fear.

I like to say worry is like sitting in a rocking chair, moving back and forth. It's always in motion, and it keeps us busy, but it never gets us anywhere. In fact, if we do it too long, it wears us out! When we worry, we are actually saying, "If I try hard enough, I can find a solution to my problem," and that is the opposite of trusting God.

The cause of worry is simple: It's the failure to trust God to take care of the circumstances of our lives. Most of us have spent years trying to take care of ourselves. Learning to trust God in every situation takes time, and we learn by doing it. We have to step out in faith, and as we do, we experience God's faithfulness, which makes it easier to trust Him the next time. Too often we trust our own abilities, believing we can figure out how to take care of our own problems. Yet most of the time, after all our worry and effort to go it alone, we realize we are unable to bring about suitable solutions. God, on the other hand, always has solutions for the things that worry us.

Trusting God allows us to enter His rest—a place of peace in our souls where we can enjoy life while we are waiting for Him to solve our problems. He cares for us, and He will solve our problems and meet our needs, but we have to stop thinking and worrying about them. I realize this is easier said than done, but there is no time like the present to begin learning a new way to live—without worry, anxiety, and fear. Now is the time to begin thinking and saying, "Because I am in Christ, I trust God

> *Trusting God allows us to enter a place of peace in our souls where we can enjoy life.*

completely. I have no need to worry!" The more you develop this victorious mindset, the more you will find yourself choosing trust over worry.

IT'S A MATTER OF FOCUS

Whatever we focus on becomes bigger and bigger in our minds, and it is possible for things to seem much bigger than they really are. When we worry, we focus on our problems; we meditate on them as we continually roll them over and over in our minds. When we are anxious about things, we also talk about them incessantly, because what is in our hearts eventually comes out of our mouths (Matthew 12:34). The more we think and talk about our problems, the larger they become in our minds. A relatively small matter can grow into a huge issue merely because we focus on it too much. Instead of meditating on the problem, we can meditate on the faithfulness of God and remind ourselves that we have no need to worry.

Now is a good time to remind yourself that you can choose your own thoughts. I have heard many people say, "I just can't help it—I am a worrier." The truth is that they chose to worry because they did not know how to trust God. Just as we become good at worrying because we practice it, we can also become good at trusting God if we practice it. Our first response in any situation should be to trust God, not to worry.

The enemy does not want us to grow in faith; he wants us to be filled with worry, anxiety, and fear. He works hard to distract us from God by encouraging us to focus excessively on our circumstances. We should develop the habit of letting what is in our hearts become more real to us than what we see, think, or feel. For example, my heart knows I can trust God completely, but my head often tells me to worry. I have had to learn to override the worry in my mind with the trust in my heart.

> *Let what is in our hearts become more real to us than what we see, think, or feel.*

If Satan can get us to think about what is wrong or what could go wrong with a situation, he can keep us from focusing on trusting God. This is why Hebrews 12:2 instructs us to look away from all that distracts us and look to Jesus. If we fix our gaze on God, think about Him, and speak of His goodness, we focus on faith. As we use our faith, it grows. As we take steps to trust God, we experience His faithfulness, which in turn encourages us to have greater faith. As our faith develops and grows, our problems have less power over us and we worry less.

We can choose to think about what God can do instead of what we cannot do. If we continually think about the difficulty of our situations, we may end up in despair and feel unable to find a way out. We feel trapped, and then it is easy to panic and begin to take irrational actions that exacerbate the problem. God always provides us with a way out of our troubles (1 Cor. 10:13). Even though you may not see the way out right now, one does exist, and God will reveal it as you trust Him.

GET SOME REST

Jesus lived a life of perfect peace. He never worried about anything, and He does not want us to worry, either. He says:

> Are you tired? Worn out? Burned out on religion? Come to me. Get away with me and you'll recover your life. I'll show you how to take a real rest. Walk with me and

work with me—watch how I do it. Learn
the unforced rhythms of grace. I won't lay
anything heavy or ill-fitting on you. Keep
company with me and you'll learn to live
freely and lightly.

Matthew 11:28–30 MSG

Living freely and lightly in the "unforced
rhythms of grace" sounds good, doesn't it? I'm
sure you have had enough heavy stuff in your
life. I have, too, and I want to be free. It is actually quite refreshing to realize that I don't need
to know everything about everything, nor do
you. We need to get comfortable saying, "I don't
know the answer to this dilemma, and I'm not
going to worry about anything, because God is
in control, and I trust Him. I'm going to rest
in Him and live freely and lightly!" When we're
overloaded with the cares of life—struggling,
laboring, and worrying—we need a mental and
emotional vacation. Our minds need to rest

from thinking about our problems, and our emotions need to rest from being upset. Worry isn't restful at all. In fact, it steals rest and the benefits of rest from us. So next time you feel you are carrying a heavy load in your mind or you find yourself worried and anxious, remember, you can live freely and lightly. All you have to do is rest in God.

RELEASE THE WEIGHT OF WORRY

It is one thing to know we should not worry but quite another to actually stop doing it. One way I learned to let go of worry was to finally realize how utterly useless it is. Let me ask you:

- How many problems have you solved by worrying?
- How much time have you spent worrying about things that never even happened?

- Has anything ever gotten any better as a result of your worrying about it? (Of course not!)

The Bible is full of sound, proven advice for dealing with worry. For example, in the Old Testament, the prophet Jeremiah writes: "Blessed is the one who trusts in the Lord, whose confidence is in him. They will be like a tree planted by the water....It has no worries in a year of drought and never fails to bear fruit" (Jer. 17:7–8). And in the New Testament, the apostle Paul teaches us to be anxious for nothing, but in all circumstances to make our prayer requests known to God with thanksgiving (Phil. 4:6). He then encourages us by saying that the peace of God will fill our hearts and minds (Phil. 4:7).

The instant you begin to worry or feel anxious, give your concern to God in prayer. Release the weight of it and totally trust Him to either show you what to do or to take care of it Himself. Prayer is a powerful force against worry. When you're under pressure, it's always best to pray about it instead of fret or talk about it excessively.

Prayer is the blueprint for a successful life. During His time on Earth, Jesus prayed. He entrusted everything to God—even His reputation and His life. We can do the same. Don't complicate your communication with God. Just have confidence in simple, believing prayer.

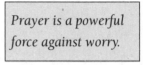

Prayer is a powerful force against worry.

Refusing to worry and releasing your cares to God completely will eventually form a new mindset that will enable you to trust Him with ease. You will habitually look for what is good and magnify it. As you learn to pray about everything and worry about nothing, you'll find yourself enjoying your life more and more.

THINK, THEN ACT

1. What do you worry about most? How can you release your worry and concern to God?

....

....

2. Do you need a mental and emotional rest? How can you put your mind at ease today?

....

....

3. What specific verses or passages from God's Word will you meditate on to help you stop worrying? Matthew 11:28–30, Philippians 4:6–7, and Jeremiah 17:7–8 are all good options.

....

....

Because I am in Christ

I Am Content and Emotionally Stable

Godliness with contentment is great gain.

1 Timothy 6:6

One of the greatest things God has done in my life is helping me become emotionally stable and consistently content, meaning continually satisfied with who God created me to be and what He has chosen to give me. It was a long journey, and I admit that it was not easy, but nothing is more tormenting than being controlled emotionally by outside forces. I look back and realize how much time and energy I wasted over the years being upset about things over which I was powerless.

In every aspect of life, Jesus is our example—and Jesus was emotionally stable. The Bible actually refers to Him as "the Rock," and we can depend on Him to be solid, steady, and stable—the same—all the time. We can count on Him to be the same today as He was yesterday and the same tomorrow as He is today (Heb. 13:8). He is not in one kind of mood one day and in another mood the next. He is always faithful, loyal, mature, and true to His Word. Being able to depend on Jesus' stability and consistency is part of what makes a relationship with Him seem attractive to us.

Part of the appeal of stability and content-ment is the fact that they enable us to enjoy our lives. None of us likes to have moments or days when emotions sink and we sit around in self-pity, filled with negative thoughts. We don't enjoy ourselves when we are in that condition, and no one else enjoys us, either. In addition, being in close relationship with anyone who is discontent, not dependable, and moody is extremely difficult. We can spend all of our time trying to keep them happy instead of being free to enjoy our own lives unless we realize we are not helping them by catering to their moods.

I have discovered that I like myself better when I am stable and consistently content, and I believe the same is true for you. Becoming emotionally stable and learning to be content are important elements of living a powerful life. As you grow in these qualities, you'll find yourself strengthened as never before.

> *Becoming emotionally stable and learning to be content are important elements of living a powerful life.*

EMOTIONS NEED TO BE MANAGED

We all have emotions, and we always will. They are part of being human. Since this is true, I believe emotional stability should be one of the main goals of every believer. We should seek God to learn how to manage our emotions—feelings of happiness, sadness, anger, fear, love, and others—and not allow them to manage us.

I've seen emotional people defined in many ways. Some say they are "easily affected with or stirred by emotion." Others say they are those "who display emotion" or those "with a tendency to rely on or place too much value on emotion" or "whose conduct is ruled by emotion rather than reason." I couldn't agree more with these definitions, and I want to add several personal observations I have made about people who are not stable emotionally:

- A person who lives by emotions lives without principle.
- We cannot be spiritual (walk in the Spirit) and be led by emotions.
- Emotions won't go away, but you can learn to manage them.

- We all have emotions, but you can't always rely on them.

I urge you to make emotional maturity a priority in your life. If you do not believe you are doing a good job managing your emotions, begin to pray and ask God to help you grow and mature in your emotions. I also encourage you to learn what situations or circumstances upset you the most or prompt you to behave emotionally and watch out for those temptations.

To help you get started, let me mention several Bible verses about stability:

- Jeremiah 17:8 and Psalm 1:3 both instruct us to be like trees firmly planted.
- First Peter 5:8–9 teaches us to be well-balanced and temperate (self-controlled) to keep Satan from devouring us. According to these verses, if we want to withstand him, we need to be rooted,

established, strong, immovable, and determined.

- Philippians 1:28 tells us to be constantly fearless when Satan comes against us.
- Psalm 94:13 says God wants to give us power to stay calm in adversity.

I encourage you to meditate on these verses and allow them to become ingrained in your thinking.

STOP THE ROLLER COASTER

I believe some of life's greatest challenges involve or result from the ups and downs of our emotions. Instead of constantly feeling that we are on an emotional roller coaster, which only exhausts us, we need to become stable, solid, steadfast, persevering, determined people. Renewing our minds to believe that we are stable and content will help us get started.

People who allow their emotions to rule over

them will not ever become the people they were meant to be. It does no good to merely wish they were not so emotional. None of us will ever be totally rid of emotions. We don't need to eliminate emotions from our lives, but we must learn to manage and control them—not allow them to have power over us. Emotions are not all bad—some of them are very enjoyable—but they are rather fickle.

> *We don't need to eliminate emotions from our lives, but we must learn to manage and control them.*

Feelings change from day to day, hour to hour, and sometimes even moment to moment. Not only do they change, but they lie. For example, you may be in a crowd of people and *feel* everybody is talking about you, but that doesn't mean they are. You may *feel* nobody understands you, but that doesn't mean they don't. You may *feel* you are not well liked, or that you're unappreciated or even mistreated, but that doesn't mean it is true. If you want to be a mature, disciplined, well-balanced person, you must be determined not to walk according to what you feel.

I believe there are two ways to become content and emotionally stable: patience and self-control.

Patience

God wants us to use wisdom, and wisdom encourages patience. It says, "Wait until your emotions settle down before you say or do anything. Then check to make sure you truly believe what you plan to do is the right course of action." Emotions push us to make quick decisions or do things in a hurry, while patience urges us to wait until we have the fullest possible understanding of a situation and the wisest way to handle it. Part of maturity is being able to slow down, step back from a situation, and view it from God's perspective. Then, we can chart our way forward based on what we *know* instead of what we *feel*.

Patience is also an aspect of contentment. It depicts people who are content or willing to wait for things instead of demanding them immediately—simply because they want them.

Self-control

You will find a chapter dedicated to discipline and self-control later in this book, so I will comment on self-control only briefly here. God's gift of free will means we can choose what we will do and will not do. When we allow our old sin nature to rule us, we will follow our emotions. But when we allow the new nature God gave us when we were born again to rule, we will be able to demonstrate self-control, which is a fruit of the Holy Spirit (Gal. 5:22–23). As believers, we have self-control and we can develop and strengthen it by using it.

Exercising self-control is a form of freedom, not a type of bondage. It will keep you from being a slave to your emotions and set you free to do what you know is wise. It will help you be what you say you want to be, it will cause you to feel better about yourself, and it will increase your self-respect. When you do not allow your emotions to control you, you will notice that you even have more energy.

Self-control will also help you make wise choices. When faced with decisions, practice self-control and wait until you have a clear answer before taking a step you might regret. Remember to be led by peace, not excitement. Emotions

> *Exercising self-control is a form of freedom, not a type of bondage.*

can be wonderful when managed and handled in a godly way, but they must not be allowed to prevail over wisdom and self-control.

THINK YOUR WAY TO STABILITY

You can think yourself into emotional stability and consistent contentment. Stop meditating on negative or disturbing things, getting upset, and then thinking and talking about how unstable and discontent you are and repeating that cycle. Instead, start thinking and saying, "I am emotionally stable and consistently content. No matter what is going on in my circumstances, I am able to remain calm and loving while I trust God to take care of it."

Let me ask you: How do you see yourself? What do you want to be? Where do you want to be in your spiritual growth this time next year? Make some decisions and start ordering your life instead of letting circumstances order you. Come into

> *No matter what is going on, I am able to remain calm and loving while I trust God to take care of it.*

agreement with God and His Word. Think what He thinks and say what He says. Will it take time? Yes, it definitely won't happen overnight and may take months or years. Will it be easy? Probably not, but it will be worth it. Will you ever backslide in your commitment to think and say positive things? Most likely, but when you fall, all you have to do is get up and try again.

Keep thinking about how wonderful it will be to get off the roller coaster of emotions that make you joyful one day and suddenly steal your joy the next. Up one moment and down the next…up and down…up and down! This is not the way God wants you to live. It does not reflect the life His Son died to give you. Take steps today to embrace and enjoy the life He has for you—and that includes being content and emotionally stable.

THINK, THEN ACT

1. On a scale of 1 to 10, how would you rate your own emotional stability and contentment? How can you improve?

....

....

2. In what area do you need to practice patience and exercise self-control in your life right now? What specific steps will you take in this area?

....

....

3. In what ways do you want to grow in emotional stability? For example, do you want to become more patient, more peaceful, more content, or more secure in who you are?

....

....

Because I am in Christ

God Meets All My Needs Abundantly

Beloved, I pray that you may prosper in all things and be in health, just as your soul prospers.

3 JOHN 2 NKJV

Developing what I call an abundant mindset—one that believes God will always provide whatever we need in every situation—is very important. This is God's promise throughout Scripture, and part of His nature is to provide for His children. In fact, in the Old Testament, one of the Hebrew names of God is "Jehovah-Jireh," which means "The Lord Our Provider." You and I are God's children. He is our Father, and He delights in providing for us just as natural parents delight in helping their children.

Dave and I have four children. They love us, we love them, and so we share all we have with them. We could not even imagine leaving them in need while we enjoy abundance—and God is certainly much better at parenting than we are.

God owns everything and is able to do anything. Psalm 24:1 says, "The earth is the Lord's, and everything in it." And in Psalm 50:10–12, God Himself says:

> For every animal of the forest is mine, and the cattle on a thousand hills. I know every bird in the mountains, and the insects in the fields are mine. If I were hungry, I would not tell you, for the world is mine, and all that is in it.

Clearly, all the resources of heaven and earth are at God's disposal, and there is nothing we need that He cannot provide. He loves us and wants to take care of us. If we love Him and do our best to progressively learn and obey His ways, He will make sure our needs are met. In fact, there is no one He would rather share His blessings with than His children.

MORE THAN MONEY

Paul promised the believers who partnered with him in his ministry that God would liberally supply all of their needs according to His riches in glory in Christ Jesus (Phil. 4:19). He didn't promise God would give them everything they wanted, but he did assure them God would meet their every need.

Many times, we think of needs in terms of the basic necessities of life—food, shelter, clothing, and finances to purchase these items. These represent our physical needs, but I believe God created us to need more than these essentials. Our needs are varied. We don't simply need money, nourishment, a roof over our heads, and clothes to wear. We also need wisdom, strength, health, friends, and loved ones, and we need gifts and talents and abilities to help us do what we are called to do in life. We need many things, and God is willing to meet all of our needs as we obey and trust Him.

We must believe that He wants to provide for us and develop an expectant mindset in this area.

> *We need many things, and God is willing to meet all of our needs as we obey and trust Him.*

The people to whom Paul wrote in Philippians helped him financially. They were obeying the law of sowing and reaping (Gal. 6:7). We cannot expect to reap where we have not sown, but when we do sow good seeds, we should indeed expect good results. This is true in every area of our lives, including health, finances, abilities, relationships, and everything else that pertains to our well-being.

If we sow good seeds by respecting our

physical bodies, eating nutritious food, drinking ample water, getting plenty of sleep, and eliminating excessive stress, we can expect to reap a harvest of good health. If we sow mercy, we will reap mercy. If we sow judgment, we will reap judgment. If we forgive, we will be forgiven. If we are friendly, we will have friends. If we are generous, we will experience generosity returned. The law of sowing and reaping is one of the simplest to understand and one that produces great power in our lives. Just think about it: If you need friends, all you have to do is be friendly!

WHAT IS PROSPERITY?

A person is never truly prosperous if all he has is a lot of money; real prosperity requires far more than that. The apostle John writes, "Beloved, I pray that you may prosper in all things and be in health, just as your soul prospers" (3 John 2

NKJV). Obviously, John had a holistic approach to prosperity, and so should we. This verse doesn't even mention money, but focuses on the body and the soul. When our bodies prosper, we are strong and physically healthy. Even if we currently have a physical ailment, we can pray for and expect healing, but we need to sow good seeds by taking care of ourselves and not abusing our bodies.

When our souls prosper, we flourish on the inside. We are at peace, we are full of joy, we are content, we live with a sense of destiny and purpose, we are growing spiritually, and we have strong, loving relationships with others.

God is a God of abundance, and He wants us to live abundant lives.

> *When our souls prosper, we flourish on the inside.*

Jesus said that He came so we could have and enjoy life in abundance and to the full (John 10:10).

IS IT WRONG TO WANT MONEY?

Wanting money is not wrong. Money is not evil; it is the *love* of money that is a root of all evil (1 Tim. 6:10). We actually need money for many things. Almost everywhere I go, money is exchanged for some goods or services. Not only does money meet our needs, but it can be used to bless others and meet their needs when they are unable to do so.

It is not God's will for wicked people to have all the money in the world while His people are constantly needy. I believe we should respect money and never waste it, and we should be good stewards of all that God gives us. Proverbs says repeatedly that we should be prudent, which means being good managers.

God also expects us to be wise investors, and if we are, He rewards us (Matt. 25:14–28). We should never love money or be greedy for gain, but we should do the best we can with what we have. We should use money in the service of

God and others, never trying to use God or anyone to get money. Money is only a small portion of prosperity, but we do need it, and asking God to supply it abundantly is not wrong.

NO MORE NEEDY MINDSETS

Many people fail to enjoy the abundance God has for them because they have an "I'm needy" mindset. They constantly fear not having enough of the resources they need. They feel they need more friends, more love, more help, and more energy. People with this "I need, I need, I need" mentality feel deprived spiritually, mentally, physically, financially, and socially.

> *Sow good seeds by helping others in need.*

Sometimes people who are plagued by feelings of neediness have truly been needy at some point in their lives. These experiences cause them to fear lack or loss, and that fear causes them to think they will never have enough, and thus they may even begin to live narrow, stingy lives. If this has happened to you, let me urge you to begin to think of yourself not as needy but as a child of God, someone He loves and for whom He is glad to provide. Sow good seeds by helping others in need, and say things that build within you the image of a person whose needs are met instead of the image of someone who is always needy. Think and say:

- All of my needs are met according to God's riches in Christ Jesus (Phil. 4:19).
- God blesses me and makes me a blessing to others (Gen. 12:2).
- I give and it is given unto me, a good measure, pressed down, shaken together, and running over (Luke 6:38).
- God richly and ceaselessly provides everything for my enjoyment (1 Tim. 6:17).
- I serve God, and He takes pleasure in my prosperity (Ps. 35:27).

We receive from God according to our faith, so developing a correct mindset toward God's provision for us is vital. We should never settle for lack in our lives, but expect abundance according to God's Word.

BE EQUIPPED TO MEET NEEDS

As I mentioned earlier, God wants us to be equipped to help people who are in need. We cannot do that if we are experiencing lack. When we don't have enough to meet our own needs and the needs of our families or others for whom we are responsible, helping people in need is very difficult. This is one reason God promises to provide for us and to do so abundantly.

To help others, we need strength, good health, and clarity of mind. We need money to help those who are struggling financially. We need clothes to be able to share with people who need them. In 2 Corinthians 9:8,

Paul teaches us that God blesses us abundantly so we will not be in need. The following verses say that God gives seed to a person who is willing to sow, meaning to give to others (2 Cor. 9:9–10). This means that if you are willing to share with others and meet their needs, God will not only meet your needs, but He will give you an abundance of supply so you will always be able to give.

I want to close this chapter with a Scripture passage that clearly and powerfully communicates what God wants to do for you. I encourage you to see it as a personal message from God to you. Let it sink into your heart and change your thinking. As you develop a mindset based on this verse, you'll find yourself more blessed than you ever thought possible.

> And therefore the Lord [earnestly] waits [expecting, looking, and longing] to be gracious to you; and therefore He lifts Himself up, that He may have mercy on

you and show loving-kindness to you. For the Lord is a God of justice. Blessed (happy, fortunate, to be envied) are all those who [earnestly] wait for Him, who expect and look and long for Him [for His victory, His favor, His love, His peace, His joy, and His matchless, unbroken companionship]!

Isaiah 30:18 AMPC

THINK, THEN ACT

1. Do you believe God loves you and wants to provide for you? How has He provided for you in the past?

....

....

2. Do you have a healthy, well-balanced attitude toward prosperity? How could you improve the way you think about prosperity and God's provision?

....

....

3. Has being needy at some time in your life developed a fear in you that you will never have enough? If so, how can you break free from that belief?

....

....

Because I am in Christ

I Pursue Peace with God, Myself, and Others

Seek peace and pursue it.

PSALM 34:14

have reached the point where I don't believe life is really worth living without peace, and that drives me to pursue peace in all areas. I spent many years frustrated and struggling in my relationships with God, myself, and other people, and I refuse to live that way now. The Amplified Bible, Classic Edition version of Psalm 34:14 says we are to "crave peace," and I can truthfully say that I do crave it. I value peace today more than ever, and I do everything I can to keep peace in every area of my life.

Psalm 34:14 says we are to *pursue* peace. *To pursue* means to actively go after something. People can chase after all kinds of things, but I believe one of the most worthwhile pursuits for anyone is to intentionally seek peace and do whatever is necessary to have peace with God, ourselves, and others.

PEACE WITH GOD

Being at peace with God begins with recognizing that we are sinners in need of a Savior. We simply need to ask Him to forgive us of our sins and believe that in His death, He took upon Himself the punishment we deserved for them. Then we receive Him into our hearts, accepting the gift of forgiveness He freely provides. Once we have received Him as Lord and Savior, we begin the journey of turning away from sinful lifestyles and learning to live as God asks us to live.

We maintain peace with God by never

attempting to hide sin. We must always maintain a clear conscience before God and keep open, honest communication with Him. When we make mistakes, we should never withdraw from Him, but we should draw near because only He can restore us. To *repent* means to change our minds, turn away from sin and return to the highest place. God is not surprised by our weaknesses and failures. Actually, He knew the mistakes we would make before we made them. All we need to do is admit those faults, and He is faithful to forgive us continually of all sin (1 John 1:9).

> *God is not surprised by our weaknesses and failures.*

To be at peace with God we must try to obey Him to the best of our ability. We will not arrive at perfection as long as we are in our earthly bodies, but we can have perfect hearts toward God and try our best every day to please Him. I like to say, "Do your best, and God will do the rest."

PEACE WITH YOURSELF

If you don't have a healthy relationship with yourself, you will struggle to have healthy relationships with God and others. Many times, though, people focus more on their external relationships than on their internal relationship with themselves because they have never even realized that they have a relationship with themselves.

One of the best ways to evaluate your relationship with yourself is to pay attention to the way you think about yourself and to what you say about yourself. If you constantly think about your faults or find yourself wondering, "What is wrong with me?" your relationship with yourself probably is not very healthy. Similarly, if you hear yourself talking about your weaknesses or putting yourself down, those words indicate that your relationship with yourself needs to improve.

Let me be quick to say that everyone has weaknesses, and that is okay. Having areas of weakness is part of being human, and our weaknesses give God a chance to show His power through us and in our lives. God accepts us and helps us in our weaknesses. So, while it is wise to be aware of them, it is foolish to focus on them excessively, because when we think too much about what we cannot do, we set ourselves up for defeat.

When we are constantly negative about ourselves, even in the privacy of our thoughts, that lack of internal peace is likely to show itself externally. If we don't like ourselves, we won't like much of anything and we will find reasons not to build relationships with others. However, if we can relax about ourselves, accept that we are not perfect, and realize that we are works in progress and that God is helping us day by day, then we can usually relax about life in general.

God created you. He has a great plan for your life, a plan that *only* you can

> *God has a great plan for your life, a plan that only you can fulfill.*

fulfill. He made you special and unique, unlike anyone else, and He loves and accepts you unconditionally. These truths form the foundation of a healthy relationship with yourself, and I encourage you to meditate on them often.

PEACE WITH OTHERS

A totally stress-free human relationship probably doesn't exist, but there are certain ways to improve our relationships and allow us to be at peace with others. I believe these four steps will help you reach the goal of enjoying peace with people.

Step 1: Adjust Your Expectations

Develop and maintain peace with God and peace with yourself. Only then will you develop a mindset that allows you to have peace with all types of people. In addition, ask God to help you see people as He sees them and to give you a heart of love for them. Pray that He will help you break free from unrealistic expectations of others. Conflict and strife often plague relationships simply because some people expect others to think, say, or do things they cannot or will not think, say, or do. If we can have balanced expectations of people, we can greatly increase our peace with them.

Step 2: Realize That Nobody's Perfect

The first expectation you may need to adjust is the expectation that people will be perfect, or even close to perfect. They won't. Only Jesus is perfect; all human beings fall short of perfection in many ways. Let me urge you not to waste your energy trying to make the impossible possible. People have faults, and there is no way around that. No matter who you are in relationship with, there will be times when they will disappoint you, so plan on forgiving frequently.

Step 3: Appreciate Differences

Don't expect everyone to be like you, because no one will be. Discovering that we are each born with a God-given temperament and that we are all unique was quite an eye-opener to me. Years ago, I learned that each individual's

> *Accept each person in your life as an individual designed specifically by God.*

personality is a combination of temperament given at birth and life events or experiences. This means no one is exactly like anyone else.

You can greatly increase peace in your relationships by simply choosing to accept each person in your life as an individual designed specifically by God and giving them freedom to be who they are.

Step 4: Encourage

Everyone loves to be with people who celebrate and notice their strengths and choose to ignore their weaknesses. We all love to be encouraged and made to feel really good about ourselves, and we hate to be around negative, discouraging people who call attention to our faults.

Being encouraging is part of being a more positive person. Be careful of your thoughts about people. Uncomplimentary or critical thoughts usually don't limit themselves to the mind. They tend to slip out of the mouth, and that is harmful to relationships. Instead, look for and magnify the good in every person both in your mind and with your words.

ACTIVELY PURSUE PEACE

If we want to live in harmony with others, we must adapt to people and things. I can assure you that I had no interest in adapting to anything or anyone. I did want them to adapt to me, but in my pride, I didn't even consider that I needed to change or accommodate them in any way, so my life and relationships remained in turmoil. After many years, I finally became willing to do whatever I needed to do to have peace, and learning how to adapt was number one on God's list for me. I have discovered that having my way all the time is not really as important as I once thought it was. Now, I actually enjoy the freedom of not having to have my way. Yes, I said the *freedom* of not having to have my own way. My flesh may be uncomfortable for a short while when I adapt to someone or something that is not really what I want, but I feel great inside because I know I have followed the law of love and done my part to pursue peace.

Adapting to others does not mean that we let them control us or that we become doormats for the world to walk on. There are times when we need to stand firm no matter who gets upset, but there are also many times when we make mountains out of molehills and give up our peace over things that are petty. Will you make a commitment to be a maker and maintainer of peace? Will you examine all of your relationships—with God, yourself, and others—and do everything you can to live in peace?

To me the most important point in this chapter is that we must *pursue* peace. Most people want peace, but they don't do what they need to in order

> *Will you make a commitment to be a maker and maintainer of peace?*

to have it. The first step is to develop the mind-set that you *will* live in peace with God, yourself, and others. As you remind yourself of that commitment and act on it, you will find yourself becoming more and more dissatisfied with turmoil. You will pursue peace!

THINK, THEN ACT

1. Are you at peace with God, yourself, and others? If not, what truths have you learned in this chapter that could help you begin to increase the level of peace in your relationships?

....

....

2. How do you need to reset your expectations of God, yourself, and others so that you will not struggle with disappointments in relationships?

....

....

3. What practical steps can you take to actively pursue peace with God, yourself, and other people?

....

....

Because I am in Christ

I Live in the Present and Enjoy Each Moment

This is the day the Lord has made; we will rejoice and be glad in it.

PSALM 118:24 NKJV

We need to enjoy every moment of our lives and stay focused on the present. We can't dwell on the past or look too far into the future. The current moment is God's gift to us right now, so we need to fully live in it and enjoy it. Every minute we live is a gift from God, and learning to live in the present can transform our lives and help us enjoy them in brand new ways.

Please remember this: Any day you waste is one you will never get back. Make every day count!

KEYS TO ENJOYING THE PRESENT MOMENT

Do you believe God wants you to enjoy your life? Of course He does! In fact, part of God's will for you is to enjoy every moment He gives you. I am sure of this because His Word says so in many places. As just one example, King Solomon, who is considered the wisest man who ever lived, writes in Ecclesiastes 2:24: "There is nothing better for a person than that he should eat and drink and find enjoyment in his toil. This also, I saw, is from the hand of God" (ESV).

Learning to live in the present and enjoy each moment can be a challenge for some people, and it can take time. In this chapter, I want to share with you some specific keys that have helped me learn to live in the present moment and enjoy my life. I believe that if you'll put them into practice in your life, they'll help you, too.

Give Yourself to What You Are Doing

When the term *multitasking* first became popular, everyone seemed to want to do it. Many job descriptions suddenly included phrases such as "must be able to multitask," and they still do. While there are certainly times a person must juggle more than one thing at a time, I am not sure multitasking serves us well in everyday life, and I don't think it should become a normal way to live. In fact, I think trying to do too many things at once creates stress and prevents us from enjoying any of them. Some people are able to do several things at once and still stay calm and focused, but even they have their limits. Doing too much at once often creates stress, confusion, and frustration—which keep us from enjoying anything.

I want to challenge you to stop trying to multitask excessively and learn to give yourself to what you are doing. Commit to do one thing at a time, concentrate on it, and determine to enjoy it. It's certainly fine to read a book while you sit in a waiting room before an appointment, but I encourage you to begin to resist the urge to simultaneously do more than one thing that requires brainpower or your full attention. For example, don't talk on the phone while paying bills online. Don't make a list of weekend home improvement projects while attending a business meeting. And definitely don't put on makeup, check social media, or send emails or text messages while driving.

> *Commit to do one thing at a time, concentrate on it, and determine to enjoy it.*

Breaking the bad habit of excessive multitasking may sound easy, but it is actually quite difficult in our society, so be determined to form new, balanced habits in this area. This book is about learning to control your thinking so you can develop healthy mindsets, and the art of focusing on what you are doing is a vital part of that goal.

Take a deep breath, slow down, and be determined to only do what you can do peacefully and enjoyably.

Become Childlike in Your Approach to God

Acting like an adult is a good thing in most cases. But we are to approach God as little children—not being child*ish*, but child*like*. One thing is certain: Little children can easily find a way to enjoy whatever they are doing. If you approach God in a childlike way, you can enjoy your relationship with Him and all that you do.

Let me encourage you to approach God with a childlike trust that does not have to understand the "why" behind everything. Have simple faith, pray simple prayers, be quick to repent, and be quick to receive God's help. Believe God is good. If you need forgiveness, ask God for it, receive it by faith, and don't waste your time feeling guilty and condemned. With this kind of simplicity in your relationship with God, you'll find yourself growing spiritually and enjoying Him more than ever. One of the worthiest

> *Have simple faith, pray simple prayers, be quick to repent, and be quick to receive God's help. Believe God is good.*

and most rewarding goals you could set for your life would be to enjoy God at all times and in everything you do.

Enjoy People

We cannot enjoy the present moment if we don't learn to enjoy all different types of people, because many of our moments include people. I recently read that most of our unhappiness is caused from people not being what we want them to be or doing what we want them to do, and I agree. I have found it helpful to realize that even though some people may annoy me, God loves them very much and wants me to have a good attitude and a heart of love toward everyone.

God has created all kinds of people with

many different temperaments and personalities, and I truly believe He enjoys them all. In fact, He seems to delight in variety. If you have never thought about this, take a little time and look around you. God created variety, and what He has created is good, so I urge you to accept those who are different from you and learn to enjoy them as God does.

Enjoy a Balanced Life

I truly believe that maintaining a life of balance is one of our biggest challenges. I encourage you to regularly examine your life and ask yourself honestly if you have allowed any area to get out of balance. Are you doing too much or too little of anything? A lack of balance could be the root cause of not enjoying life.

I have not always lived a balanced life, but I thank God for helping me reach the point where I do stay balanced now—most of the time. I encourage you to do the same. Balance your activities and vary your routine. Balance work

> *Balance work with rest and fun.*

with rest and fun. Don't do the same things all the time or overdo anything. That will help you avoid burnout and be able to enjoy everything.

Let Go of the Past

Your past can be an unbearably heavy load when you try to carry it into your present. The way to let go of it is to stop thinking about it. Get it off of your mind and out of your conversation. Satan will remind you of your past because he wants you to stay stuck in it, but please remember that you can choose your thoughts. You do not have to think about everything that falls into your mind.

Holding on to your past will keep you from enjoying your present and looking forward to your future. If you struggle with guilt, condemnation, shame, blame, or regret about your past, God will forgive you and set you free if you simply ask Him.

Choose Your Battles

I believe one of the best ways to enjoy the present moment and avoid undue stress is to refuse to let every little thing upset you. In other words, choose your battles, and don't make mountains out of molehills. Before you devote time, energy, and emotion to an issue or a situation, ask yourself two questions:

- How important is this situation?
- How much of my time, effort, and energy is really appropriate for me to put into this?

Know what truly matters in life, and focus on those things. Learn to discern the difference between major matters and minor matters.

Realize That You Cannot Meet Everyone's Expectations

We all have many different relationships, and most people expect something from us. Some expectations people have of us are reasonable, and we are responsible for meeting them—such as caring for our children. Other expectations are unreasonable—such as when people expect us to do things for them when they are capable of doing those things for themselves but simply do not want to make the effort. When we meet everyone's expectations, we become exhausted. We are also pleasing people rather than pleasing God, and we become ineffective. We all want others to be pleased with us, but we must also realize that they frequently have unrealistic or inappropriate expectations. We are wise to seek God so we can understand which expectations He would have us meet and which ones we do not need to meet.

Don't Wait to Enjoy Yourself

Our ministry hosts a number of conferences each year, and I do a lot of speaking and teaching at each one. I used to view these events as work, as part of my job. Every time I did a conference,

I thought, *This is my work, and when my work is over, I will enjoy myself.* After several years, I began to think about how much time I spend in the pulpit, and realized that if I don't enjoy it, I will not have much time left to enjoy anything. So, I decided to have fun while I work. This is one way I have learned to enjoy every moment.

Find ways to enjoy the present moments in your life. Certainly, learning to be happy while you work may be one way, but there are many others. Begin now to think about what you can do to find more joy

> *Find ways to enjoy the present moments in your life.*

in every experience. The present moment is all we're guaranteed, so don't wait until later—until you get married, until you retire, until you go on vacation, until your children finish college—to enjoy life. Nobody knows what is going to happen next in their lives or in the world. You are alive now, so maximize it, embrace it, and celebrate it.

THINK, THEN ACT

1. What are three childlike traits that you could practice in your relationship with God?

....

....

2. Do you live a balanced life? Where do you need to improve, and how can you do better?

....

....

3. Think about your current battles. Which ones do you need to walk away from, and which ones are worth fighting?

....

....

Because I am in Christ

I Am Disciplined and Self-controlled

No discipline seems pleasant at the time, but painful. Later on, however, it produces a harvest of righteousness and peace for those who have been trained by it.

HEBREWS 12:11

I truly believe that a disciplined life is a powerful life. Learning to be disciplined and to practice self-control will keep you from laziness and excess, and will help you stay focused and productive. It will require you to make an effort, but the reward will be worth the work. A disciplined life begins with a disciplined mind. We must be able to set our mind and keep it set concerning our desires and goals.

LIBERTY WITH LIMITS

The apostle Paul understood discipline and wrote about it in several of his letters. In 1 Corinthians 6:12, he observes, "Everything is permissible (allowable and lawful) for me; but not all things are helpful (good for me to do, expedient and profitable when considered with other things). Everything is lawful for me, but *I will not become the slave of anything or be brought under its power*" (AMPC, emphasis mine).

Discipline is the price of freedom and the door to liberation. When we are not disciplined, we fall under the power of things that should have no control over us. For example, when we don't discipline ourselves to eat health-ily, we become slaves to fats, sugars, and other substances that are detrimental to our physical health. When we do not practice self-control with our finances, we fall under the power of debt, and our indebtedness can literally keep us from doing what we want or need to do in life. When we do not discipline ourselves to get enough rest, we become slaves to fatigue, which makes us grouchy, prone to mistakes, and tired when we need to be energetic.

The enemy wants to control our lives by influencing as much of our thinking as possible, but we do not have to let him do it. Just as we have to be educated about how to think as God wants us to think, we also have to learn to resist the enemy as he tries to influence our thoughts. The key to overcoming him is learning to discipline our thinking, which starts with thinking and believing that we are disciplined.

> *Discipline is the price of freedom and the door to liberation.*

When we truly understand the power, liberty, joy, and victory that discipline brings to our lives, we will embrace it eagerly. In many areas, especially in our thinking, it makes the difference between a happy life and a miserable life—a life of bondage to the enemy or a life of freedom in Christ. Always remember that discipline is a tool God gives us to help us reach our goals. It is our friend, something to be embraced and used daily.

WINNING OVER A WANDERING MIND

One reason disciplining our minds is so important is that they can change so quickly. One moment, we may be calm, peaceful, sure of ourselves, and confident in God. An hour later, we may be anxious, worried, insecure, and full of doubt. I have certainly experienced these kinds of ups and downs at times in my life, and these emotions are always rooted in the way I think.

When the enemy has established certain ways of thinking in our minds, he does not give up his ground easily. We must be willing to not only start thinking properly but also be disciplined to keep it up until we have victory. If you have spent years allowing your mind to wander in all sorts of directions, retraining it will take time, but the effort you invest in it will yield amazing dividends.

Lots of people struggle with indecision and other challenges in their minds because they have not disciplined themselves concerning their thoughts. People who can't seem to concentrate long enough to make a decision often wonder if something is wrong with their mind. However, the inability to concentrate and make decisions can be the result of years of letting the mind do whatever it wants to do rather than disciplining it. This is often the sign and the result of a stronghold (established way of thinking) the enemy has constructed in a person's mind.

For me, tearing down the enemy's mental strongholds took time, but it did happen, and it can happen for you. It wasn't easy for me, so don't be discouraged if it takes time and effort

> *Ask God to help you, and trust Him to give you victory in due time.*

for you, too. Ask God to help you, and trust Him to give you victory in due time.

It Takes Practice

Training our minds to be disciplined takes practice. One thing I'm learning is to stop allowing my mind to wander during conversations. Sometimes Dave is talking to me and I listen for a while, and then suddenly realize I haven't heard one word he has spoken because I allowed my mind to wander to something else. For years, when this sort of thing happened, I pretended to know exactly what Dave was saying. Now I simply stop and ask, "Would you repeat that? I let my mind wander, and I didn't hear a thing you said." This way, I'm dealing with the problem. I'm disciplining my mind to stay on track.

I've also discovered that we all have a lot of what I call "mental roaming time"—time when we are not occupied with anything specific and our minds are free to roam around and select something to meditate on. This might be drive time, shower time, the time before falling asleep, or other times. We need to be careful to use these moments in productive ways and make sure we think about things that build character and help us grow spiritually. Next time you find your mind wandering and thinking useless thoughts, consider thinking some of these thoughts from this book instead:

- I can do whatever I need to do in life through Christ.
- God loves me unconditionally.
- I will not live in fear.
- I am difficult to offend.
- I love people, and I enjoy helping them.
- I trust God completely; I have no need to worry!
- I am content and emotionally stable.
- God meets all my needs abundantly.

- I pursue peace with God, myself, and others.
- I live in the present and enjoy each moment.
- I am disciplined and self-controlled.
- I put God first in all things.

Remember, the mind is the battlefield. It is the place where you will win or lose life's battles. Indecision, uncertainty, fear, and random "roaming" thoughts are simply results of not disciplining the mind. This lack of discipline can be frustrating and make you think, *What is wrong with me? Why can't I keep my mind on what I am doing?* But the truth is, the mind needs to be disciplined and trained to focus. You have a spirit of discipline and self-control, and it is time to start developing it.

> *Start developing your spirit of discipline and self-control.*

Ask God to help you, and then refuse to allow your mind to think about whatever it pleases. Begin today to control your thoughts and keep your mind on what you're doing, saying, or hearing. You'll need to practice for a while; breaking old habits and forming new ones always takes time. Developing discipline is never easy, but it's always worth it in the end. When you win the battle for your mind, you'll be much more decisive, more confident, and more focused. Then, you'll also be a more effective, more productive, happier person.

CONTROL YOURSELF

Self-control is closely related to discipline. I like to say that self-control and discipline are friends that will help you do what you don't want to do, so you can have what you say you want to have. According to Galatians 5:23 and 2 Timothy 1:7, God has given us the fruit of self-control. Therefore, it is inaccurate for a person to say, "I can't control myself."

To live with discipline and self-control means

to exercise restraint. Restraint is not always fun, but the Bible presents it as admirable. In Proverbs 1:15, King Solomon writes to his son about how to live with sinners all around him: "My son, do not walk in the way with them; *restrain your foot* from their path" (AMPC, emphasis mine). Proverbs 10:19 notes, "In a multitude of words transgression is not lacking, but he who *restrains his lips* is prudent" (AMPC, emphasis mine). Here, we see that restraining ourselves is part of being wise. It's also part of having good common sense, as we see in Proverbs 19:11: "Good sense makes a man *restrain his anger*, and it is his glory to overlook a transgression or an offense" (AMPC, emphasis mine).

Restraint has many benefits, and learning to practice it will serve us well in every aspect of our lives. Many people are not interested in restraint or self-control, and discipline certainly isn't a popular concept. People tend to prefer living by the motto "If it feels good, do it." The problem is, that just doesn't work! I don't believe

I am exaggerating to say the world may well be in the worst condition it has ever been in right now, and people enjoy more supposed freedom than at any other time in history. Human rights and true godly freedom are wonderful things, but to think that having freedom means we can do whatever we want to do whenever we want to do it is to invite disaster into our lives.

I believe God knew what He was talking about when He encouraged us to be disciplined. Discipline is a good thing. Increase the discipline in your life, and you'll see what I mean. Think of areas in your life that you want to improve; it could be finances, health, better organization in your life, how you think, what you talk about, or any number of things. Now say, "I am a disciplined and self-controlled person, and I will do my part to get my life in order."

THINK, THEN ACT

1. Are you living in bondage to anything, or does anything have power over you? If so, what is it?

....

....

2. Does your mind wander? If so, when? What specific thoughts will you begin to think when you realize your mind is not focused?

....

....

3. Do you believe you exercise appropriate self-control? In what area do you most need to improve your ability to restrain or discipline yourself?

....

....

MINDSET 12

Because I am in Christ

I Put God First in My Life

You shall have no other gods before me.

Exodus 20:3

I want to close this book with what I consider to be the most vital mindset we can develop: putting God first in everything. We should put Him first in all of our thoughts, words, and decisions. He loves us and wants us to have the very best lives possible. He knows that can only happen if we keep Him and His instructions to us as our number one priority at all times. I think this scripture says it all:

> For from Him and through Him and to Him are all things. [For all things originate

with Him and come from Him; all things live through Him, and all things center in and tend to consummate and to end in Him.] To Him be glory forever! Amen (so be it).

Romans 11:36 AMPC

This verse reminds me that life is all about God. When our earthly lives end, He is all that remains. The Earth and the things in it will vanish. They will simply disappear, and we will all stand before God and give an account of our lives (Rom. 14:12). This is why each of us should be careful how we live and learn to keep God first in all things.

Everything God asks us to do is for our good. His instructions are intended to show us the way to righteousness, peace, and joy. Jesus didn't die so we could have a religion, but so we can have a deep and intimate personal relationship with God through Him. Jesus wants us to live in Him, with Him, through Him, and for

Him. God created us for fellowship with Him-self through Jesus Christ.

I have realized that it is possible to receive Jesus Christ as Lord and yet never truly put Him above all else. We may want Him and what He offers but still be reluctant to give ourselves to Him for His use and

> *Jesus died so that we can have a deep and intimate personal relationship with God through Him.*

will. We are to live dedicated, consecrated lives in which God and His will are our top prior-ity. People who do not do so will never be truly content and satisfied.

TOO BUSY?

I believe that most people would like to have a great relationship with God, but they fail to realize it depends on the time they are willing to invest in getting to know Him. Some don't think it is possible to be intimate with God, and many are simply too busy with other things and allow their relationship with God to take a back seat to everything else they do. The truth is, if we think we are too busy to make spending time with God a priority, then we are simply too busy. I believe anyone's success in business, in ministry, or in everyday life is directly linked to the place of importance they give God in their daily lives.

WITH ALL YOUR HEART

We miss the greatest experience in life if we never really get to know God personally. We must seek Him daily. The apostle Paul said that his *determined purpose* was to know God and the power that flowed out from His resurrection (Phil. 3:10). This is a worthy endeavor for anyone.

Jesus plainly told us what our number one goal and priority should be. When the Pharisees asked Him what was the most important commandment of all, He responded, "Love the Lord your God with all your heart and with all your soul and with all your mind" (Matt. 22:37). In other words, we can't love God only when we need Him to help us; we can't love Him only when it's popular or convenient for us; we shouldn't just pay attention to Him when we're at church or because we think He might punish us if we don't. We are to love Him from our hearts—not out of fear or obligation. And we are to love Him passionately and devotedly, more than we love anyone or anything else. That's what "with all your heart" means.

PRACTICAL WAYS TO PUT GOD FIRST

The idea of putting God first is appealing to many people, but they are not sure how to do it in practical ways. Let me suggest three simple ways you can do it.

1. Ask

First, ask God to give you the desire to put Him first. Some people have a great desire to give God first place in their lives, while others wrestle with it. No matter how you feel about putting God first—a strong commitment or still struggling—wanting Him to be your first priority is important, because desire is the fuel that enables you to keep growing in Him. It makes you want to be in His presence, keeps you disciplined in your spiritual life, and helps you stay focused as you pray and read God's Word.

2. Be Disciplined

Second, you'll have to exercise spiritual discipline. You read about discipline in the previous chapter, and it applies as much to your spiritual life as it does to other areas of life. The spiritual part of you wants and needs to spend quality time with God, but your flesh needs to be disciplined to do it. It needs to form new habits, including spending time in God's Word and in prayer, praising and worshipping God, serving Him, and being generous as He leads you to bless and care for others. These spiritual disciplines keep your spiritual life strong and vibrant. Make the effort to practice them, and you'll see what I mean.

> *Spiritual disciplines keep your spiritual life strong and vibrant.*

3. Educate Yourself

Third, educate yourself concerning His ways and purposes. You certainly have to put your heart into seeking God, but you also have to put your mind into it and you have to learn things you may not know yet. Find a good, solid, Bible-based church and get involved in it. Read books; listen to sermons and teachings; take classes or go to Bible studies; attend conferences and seminars; find people who are more mature and experienced in God than you are and ask them questions that will help you grow spiritually. Investing time and money into getting the

resources you need to grow is a valuable invest-
ment that pays wonderful dividends.

ACT ON YOUR LOVE FOR GOD

We cannot simply say we love God and want to
put Him first in our lives and then expect it to
happen automatically. We must act—and we act
on our love by obeying Him. If we truly desire
to obey Him, we steadily grow in learning how
to hear His voice and choose the path He is asking us to take. I encourage you to pray daily
that you will receive from God the grace to obey
Him. Don't just try—pray!

In Exodus 24, God spoke to Moses, and
Moses recorded what He said. When he read
these words to God's people, they responded,
"All that the Lord has said we will do, and we
will be obedient" (Exod. 24:7 AMPC). Obviously,
they did not treat God's Word lightly. They
understood that they could not simply hear
what God said; they also had to obey. When I

read this passage, I get the impression the people had come to hear the Word having already decided that they wanted to learn what they were supposed to do and how they were supposed to live. Their attitude seemed to be, "No matter what God says, we will do it." If you will adopt that same mindset, your attitude will be one of prompt obedience to God—which is one way to demonstrate that He is first in your life—rather than one of procrastination and excuses.

PUT FIRST THINGS FIRST

I could not write about putting God first without mentioning Matthew 6:33 (AMPC): "But seek (aim at and strive after) first of all His kingdom and His righteousness (His way of doing and being right), and then all these things taken together will be given you besides." In other words, if we put God first, all our needs will be met, and everything else will fall into place.

The idea of putting God first appears

throughout the Bible. In the Old Testament, God's people gave what was called "firstfruits offerings"—the firsts of everything they had, including their produce, firstborn animals, first-born sons, their gold and silver. Everything. So, if a man worked as a farmer, he gave the first crops that appeared in his field to the Lord as an offering.

When we give God our firsts, we are say-ing, "Lord, I want to give this to You before I do anything else. I trust You to take care of me and meet all of my needs, and I want to honor You with the first evidence of my provision and increase. I don't want to give You my leftovers;

> *Trust God to take care of you and all of your needs.*

I want to give You my firsts, to show that You are first in my life. I'm giving You my firstfruits, and I trust You to bring more." If we give God the first of everything that comes our way, the rest is blessed.

I urge you to put God first by giving Him your firsts. Give Him the first part of each day by spending time with Him before you do anything else. Begin to schedule your day around God instead of trying to work God into your day. If we give Him the first part, He will make the rest extremely productive. Give God the first portion of your finances by not waiting to see what you have left for Him after you pay your bills. Give God the first of your attention by turning to Him for guidance before you run to your friends for advice.

God is able and willing to do more for us than we could ever ask or think (Eph. 3:20). He desires to enlarge our lives, and He wants us to enjoy Him, as well as to enjoy our lives.

> *God is able and willing to do more for us than we could ever ask or think.*

Putting God first is a choice. You have to do it deliberately. But it's a choice that brings greater blessings than you could ever imagine—peace in your heart, joy, fulfillment in life, provision for every need, and every other good thing. Put God first in your life today and every day. And watch to see what He will do!

THINK, THEN ACT

1. I want you to be totally honest with yourself and ask yourself if you've let anything get ahead of God. If you have, what changes will you make to put Him first in your life?

2. Do you give God the firsts of your time, your energy, your financial resources, and your love? How might you improve in giving Him the firsts of all you have?

3. Are you in close fellowship with God, and do you enjoy Him?

CONCLUSION

Thinking right thoughts according to God's Word is one of the most important things we should learn to do. I want to remind you that doing so will take time and that while you are on your journey, you will make mistakes. When you do, don't give up and think, *I'll never get this right.* Just keep going, because diligence always pays off in the end.

Thinking things on purpose or having what I call "think sessions" is one of the best ways to help renew your mind. This book contains twelve powerful mindsets, but there are hundreds of others that will be just as beneficial to you, so expand this list and personalize it for your own needs.

Be sure to think good things about others and yourself, remembering that thoughts turn into actions. Think positively about everything, especially your future. God has some really good things planned for you, but you need to agree with Him in order to see them become realities in your life.

My prayer is that this book has helped you and will continue to help you renew your mind so you can enjoy the wonderful life that Jesus died to give you.

If you have never received Jesus as your Savior, and you are ready to make that decision, please pray the prayer we have included on the next page. If you have any questions about how to begin your new life as a believer in Jesus, please call our office and let us help you.

Do you have a real relationship with Jesus?

God loves you! He created you to be a special, unique, one-of-a-kind individual, and He has a specific purpose and plan for your life. And through a personal relationship with your Creator—God—you can discover a way of life that will truly satisfy your soul.

No matter who you are, what you've done, or where you are in your life right now, God's love and grace are greater than your sin—your mistakes. Jesus willingly gave His life so you can receive forgiveness from God and have new life in Him. He's just waiting for you to invite Him to be your Savior and Lord.

If you are ready to commit your life to Jesus and follow Him, all you have to do is ask Him to forgive your sins and give you a fresh start in the life you are meant to live. Begin by praying this prayer . . .

Lord Jesus, thank You for giving Your life for me and forgiving me of my sins so I can have a personal relationship with You. I am sincerely sorry for the mistakes I've made, and I know I need You to help me live right. Your Word says in Romans 10:9, "If you declare with your mouth, 'Jesus is Lord,' and believe in your heart that God raised him from the dead, you will be saved" (niv). I believe You are the Son of God and confess You as my Savior and Lord. Take me just as I am, and work in my heart,

MAKING ME THE PERSON YOU WANT ME TO BE.
I WANT TO LIVE FOR YOU, JESUS, AND I AM SO GRATEFUL
THAT YOU ARE GIVING ME A FRESH START IN MY
NEW LIFE WITH YOU TODAY.
I LOVE YOU, JESUS!

It's so amazing to know that God loves us so much! He wants to have a deep, intimate relationship with us that grows every day as we spend time with Him in prayer and Bible study. And we want to encourage you in your new life in Christ.

Please visit joycemeyer.org/KnowJesus to request Joyce's book *A New Way of Living*, which is our gift to you. We also have other free resources online to help you make progress in pursuing everything God has for you.

Congratulations on your fresh start in your life in Christ! We hope to hear from you soon.

ABOUT THE AUTHOR

JOYCE MEYER is one of the world's leading practical Bible teachers. A *New York Times* bestselling author, Joyce's books have helped millions of people find hope and restoration through Jesus Christ. Joyce's program, *Enjoying Everyday Life*, airs around the world on television, radio, and the Internet. Through Joyce Meyer Ministries, Joyce teaches internationally on a number of topics with a particular focus on how the Word of God applies to our everyday lives. Her candid communication style allows her to share openly and practically about her experiences so others can apply what she has learned to their lives.

Joyce has authored more than 130 books, many of which have been translated into 155 languages. Bestsellers include *Power Thoughts*; *The Confident Woman*; *Look Great, Feel Great*; *Starting Your Day Right*; *Ending Your Day Right*;

Approval Addiction; *How to Hear from God*; *Beauty for Ashes*; and *Battlefield of the Mind*.

Joyce's passion to help hurting people is foundational to the vision of Hand of Hope, the missions arm of Joyce Meyer Ministries. Hand of Hope provides worldwide humanitarian outreaches such as feeding programs, medical care, water relief, disaster relief, human trafficking intervention and rehabilitation, and much more—always sharing the love and gospel of Christ.

JOYCE MEYER MINISTRIES

U.S. & FOREIGN OFFICE ADDRESSES

Joyce Meyer Ministries
P.O. Box 655
Fenton, MO 63026
USA
(636) 349-0303

**Joyce Meyer Ministries—
Canada**
P.O. Box 7700
Vancouver, BC V6B 4E2
Canada
(800) 868-1002

**Joyce Meyer Ministries—
Australia**
Locked Bag 77
Mansfield Delivery Centre
Queensland 4122
Australia
(07) 3349 1200

**Joyce Meyer Ministries—
England**
P.O. Box 1549
Windsor SL4 1GT
United Kingdom
01753 831102

**Joyce Meyer Ministries—
South Africa**
P.O. Box 5
Cape Town 8000
South Africa
(27) 21-701-1056

**Joyce Meyer Ministries—
Francophonie**
29 avenue Maurice Chevalier
77330 Ozoir la Ferriere
France

**Joyce Meyer Ministries—
Germany**
Postfach 761001
22060 Hamburg
Germany
+49 (0)40 / 88 88 4 11 11

**Joyce Meyer Ministries—
Netherlands**
Lorenzlaan 14
7002 HB Doetinchem
+31 657 555 9789

**Joyce Meyer Ministries—
Russia**
P.O. Box 789
Moscow 101000
Russia
+7 (495) 727-14-68

OTHER BOOKS BY JOYCE MEYER

* Study Guide available for this title

The Love Revolution

Making Good Habits, Breaking Bad Habits

Making Marriage Work (previously published as
Help Me—I'm Married!)

Me and My Big Mouth!*

The Mind Connection*

Never Give Up!

Never Lose Heart

New Day, New You

Overload

The Penny

Perfect Love (previously published as *God Is Not Mad at You*)*

Philippians: A Biblical Study

The Power of Being Positive

The Power of Being Thankful

The Power of Determination

The Power of Forgiveness

The Power of Simple Prayer

Power Thoughts

Power Thoughts Devotional

Quiet Times with God Devotional

Reduce Me to Love

The Secret Power of Speaking God's Word

The Secrets of Spiritual Power

The Secret to True Happiness

Seven Things That Steal Your Joy

Start Your New Life Today

Starting Your Day Right

BOOKS BY DAVE MEYER

Because I am in Christ...

I can do everything I need to do in life.

I am loved unconditionally.

I will not live in fear.

I am difficult to offend.

I love people and enjoy helping them.

*I trust God completely and have
no need to worry.*

I am content and emotionally stable.

God meets all my needs abundantly.

I pursue peace with God, myself, and others.

I live in the present and enjoy each moment.

I am disciplined and self-controlled.

I put God first in my life.